BIOGRAPHIES
from the KENTUCKY HERO series

To Be Greater Than Marconi:
The Nathan B. Stubblefield Story
by TRACEY D. BUCHANAN

Her Troublesome Boys:
The Lucy Furman Story
by GRETA McDONOUGH

Ring the Silver Bell:
The Alice Slone Story
by NANCY KELLY ALLEN

~

HISTORICAL FICTION
Here & Then
(a Civil War time travel tale)
by GEORGE ELLA LYON

Swing Low, Sweet Harriet
(Harriet Tubman helps organize a freedom raid)
by RHONDA HICKS RUCKER

The Pleasant Hill Series
(three books about life among the Shakers)
Road to Pleasant Hill
'Tis A Gift
Tree of Life
by REBECCA MITCHELL TURNEY & MARIE MITCHELL

~

FICTION
Callie Rose
by AMY CAUDILL HOGG

The Search for Coyote Woman
by DEBBIE MANNY MOSLEY

Swing Low, Sweet Harriet

RHONDA HICKS RUCKER

Swing Low, Sweet Harriet
RHONDA HICKS RUCKER

HISTORICAL FICTION
ISBN 978-1-934894-50-7

ACKNOWLEDGEMENTS
This book would not have been possible without the help of my husband, James "Sparky" Rucker. It was through him I first learned of Harriet Tubman's involvement in the June 1863 raid on the Combahee River. He was also the one who first read my manuscript and gave me advice and encouragement. Many thanks to Dr. Asa Gordon, who first informed my husband about the expedition. I want to give special thanks to members of my critique group: Terry Caruthers, Richard Willey and Ann Schwarz. They gave me invaluable feedback. Thanks to Benjamin Pendragon for cover photo compilation. And finally, thanks to my editor and publisher, Kate Larken.
– RHR

Cover photographs courtesy of the Library of Congress Photographs and Prints Division: LC-DIG-cwpb-00806 (digital file from original neg. of left half); LC-DIG-cwpb-00805 (digital file from original neg. of right half); LC-DIG-ppmsca-10996 (digital file from original item, front); LC-DIG-ppmsca-10997 (digital file from original item, back); LC-DIG-ppmsca-11182 (digital file from original item, front); LC-DIG-ppmsca-11183 (digital file from original item, back)
(William Gladstone Collection of African American Photographs)

Cover Photo Composite
Benjamin Pendragon

Book Design
EYE . *K*

Published in Kentucky by

www.MOTESBOOKS.com

PRINTED & BOUND IN THE USA

for
James "Sparky" Rucker

South Carolina pronunciations of place names:

Combahee — COME bee
Beaufort — BYOO furt

Chapter 1

REBEL RUMORS

South Carolina, 1863

Big **Mama stood at the table**, stirring cornbread batter. Ben tiptoed along the rear of the cabin, turned the handle of the back door, and opened it. *Creeakk!!*

"Ben!"

"Yes'm." He had forgotten to grease those hinges.

"You finished out in that barn?"

"Yes'm."

"You sure?"

"Yes'm."

"Where you going now?"

Here it comes. "Thought I'd go fishing for a spell."

Big Mama quit stirring the batter for several seconds. She turned and looked at Ben. "Remember there's cottonmouths and gators out there."

"I remember."

Big Mama was always worried about the swamp creatures. "Well you just mind yourself and be careful, you hear?"

"Yes'm."

That was easier than he thought. Maybe she realized he was getting older, or maybe she just wanted some fish to cook.

He dug out his line and pole from the shed and made his way to the Combahee River. There were still a couple of hours of daylight left, and he might get lucky.

The endless rice paddies spread out before him like a table. Tomorrow, he'd be back out there planting with all the other field hands. Ol' Man Pipkin would be standing over them with his whip in hand. April had barely begun, but the sun was already bearing down hard by midday, making work miserable. About a year ago, Ben's sister Milly had started working in the Big House. He was glad she didn't have to work the fields anymore. His little brother, Thomas, was another matter. He had to carry the water bucket to the workers.

Ben finally reached the Combahee. He found a stick on the riverbank and threw it into the water, watching it float downstream. He wondered how long it would take to reach the plantation where his mother lived. Three years ago, she had been sold to Massa Kirkland, who lived downriver on the Rosehill Plantation. It was the last time he had seen her.

Hearing a rustling noise in the grass, Ben glanced over and saw a water bird poised with its wings spread, drying its feathers. A moment later, it took off, first flapping its wings, then soaring against the gray sky. Ben watched as the bird disappeared, remembering the day his mother had been taken away. It was bad enough seeing it happen. But then he had to hear Brother James, the preacher, tell some of the old folks about it later that evening. "Weren't no warning she was being sold," he had said. "No warning at all. Massa Kirkland showed up this morning and went inside the Big House to talk to Massa Lowndes. Nobody thought nothing of it."

But Ben would never forget the moment when both men came outside and Massa Lowndes announced he was selling Mama to Massa Kirkland. Mama dropped down on the ground and cried, begging him not to sell her away from her children.

Ben had never seen Mama like that before. Massa Lowndes had explained how he needed money since times were hard. She kept crying and begging till Massa Lowndes wouldn't even look at her anymore. Mistress was standing on the porch, twisting a handkerchief in her hands, till Massa Lowndes finally told her to go inside. As Massa Kirkland drove Mama away in the carriage, she turned around, looking back at Ben standing in the road with Milly and Thomas. She held her hands out and hollered, "Ben, promise to remember me to the little ones!"

"I promise," he had said, barely able to speak. He was ten years old at the time. Milly was seven and Thomas was only four. They didn't even get to say goodbye to Mama.

Ben had tried to keep that promise. He made sure Milly and Thomas knew both Mama's names. Massa Lowndes and the white folk had called her Rabbit, but Mama hated that name. In the cabins, everybody called her Martha, the name her mother had given her.

Ben angrily grabbed another stick and threw it towards the river, but it broke off in his hand and most of it fell to the ground, never reaching the water.

Trudging a little further downstream, Ben searched among the tall grasses for a promising niche in the riverbank to throw in his line. In the distance, he heard male voices, but when he turned toward the sound, nobody was there. Scrambling up the bank, Ben found a cluster of oak trees and hid inside the shield of Spanish moss that hung almost to the ground.

The voices got louder. Two men in gray uniforms rode up on horses, then turned and faced the river, almost touching the Spanish moss in front of Ben. Lucky thing he'd left the riverbank.

"We'll be planting one here, sir."

"These are large plantations, aren't they, Captain?"

"Yes, sir."

"How many more're you planning for this area?"

"Three more, sir. One'll be downriver at the edge of this plantation by the big cypress. Another'll be up yonder just this side of the mill. And the last one at the first corner of Colonel Heyward's fence."

"Well, all ten of them better be in place by the end of this month."

"Sir, we haven't even received some of the parts from the quartermaster, yet. We won't be able to start work until..."

"Nevertheless, Captain, they need to be in place. We've got to be ready."

"Yes, sir."

They quickly rode off, and Ben realized he had been holding his breath.

Big Mama hadn't said anything about soldiers, but Ben knew they would fit into the category of cottonmouths and gators. If she found out about the soldiers, she would put a stop to his fishing. He had to tell somebody, though. Maybe Will, his best friend, was around. Ben double-checked the chicken coop and pig pen to make sure they were closed. He wandered down the row of cabins, then stopped and peeked into an open door. Small children were being herded to bed.

"Will?" Ben said.

Will was crouching at the fire and adding wood. He turned to face Ben. "You going to meeting?"

"Uh huh. Lemme talk to you."

They walked outside behind the cabin. Ben whispered, "I just got back from the Combahee. Saw some soldiers down there."

"Did they see you?"

"No. I stayed hidden."

"Wish I coulda seen 'em. Could you hear what they was saying?"

Ben nodded. "They was talking about planting something in the river."

"Planting what?"

"Don't know. They didn't say. They're putting ten things in the river, and one of them is gonna be at the spot where they was talking today. They talked about three more places—the mill, downriver at the edge of the plantation, and the corner of Colonel Heyward's fence."

"Wonder when they gonna do it," Will said.

"They're all supposed to be done by the end of the month."

"You going back to look?"

Ben nodded. "Uh huh. But I ain't telling Big Mama about it."

Will couldn't suppress his excitement. "Can I go with you?"

Just then, Brother James walked by, going to Sunday prayer meeting. The boys looked at each other.

Ben waved. "See you later." Walking toward his cabin, he remembered that he was late and didn't have any fish. Hopefully, Big Mama wouldn't ask too many questions. He wondered if anybody else had seen soldiers. Maybe they'd talk about it at the meeting tonight.

In the cabin, Big Mama had one hand firmly planted on Thomas's shoulder and the other on her hip as she tried to move Thomas. "Get yourself in bed now!"

"When do I get to stay up for meeting?" Thomas whined.

"You're too little. You're gonna make us all late." She guided him into a room where a long row of children already lay in the small cabin.

11

Big Mama came out and removed her apron. She had been cooking, and a bead of sweat was running over a prominent scar on her left cheek. She wiped her face with a rag. "Let's go, Ben."

The meeting was held in the cabin on the end—as far as possible from the Big House. The singing had already begun.

Get on board, children, children,
Get on board, children, children,
Get on board, children, children,
There's room for many a more.

Will slipped into the meeting shortly after Ben came in. After several songs, Brother James stood and said a long prayer. Ben used to think this was all there was to meeting. But he had learned it was all just a show so the white folk would think they were having church.

"Who has something to say?" Brother James looked around the circle. A small fire glowed in the center.

A tall, thin man with an angular face spoke. "I still want to know if we're supposed to be free."

A big, hulking dark man sat in the corner with a straw hat turned to one side. He glared at the thin man. "Sam, you really think the white folks would tell us if Mr. Lincoln set us free?"

"Well, Big Joe, I think there's something to that man's stories. I think he was telling the truth. I tell you one thing: I sure would like to see some of them black soldiers he was talking about. I'd join up if I could."

Big Joe snorted. "Them's only stories."

A black man had slipped onto the plantation about a month ago, telling them President Lincoln had set the slaves free in the southern states. He had also told them the Union Army was recruiting black soldiers to fight for their own freedom in a South Carolina regiment. The soldiers were just downriver near Beaufort. He had tried to persuade some of the people on Massa Lowndes' plantation to escape so they could join the regiment. The stranger's visit had created a stir.

Milly appeared in the doorway and slipped into the circle. Brother James nodded to her. "You have any news for us this week, sister?"

Milly sat up tall. She was the youngest one at the meeting, but the adults always made her feel important since she heard talk in the Big House. "Nothing much, Brother James. I didn't hear any more about Mr. Lincoln's emancipation thing. I think they try not to talk about that around us."

Things were winding down quickly tonight. Ben glanced at Uncle Minus. "You feel like telling a story tonight, Uncle Minus?"

"Oh, I don't know, Ben. This ol' rheumatis is giving me an awful go for it." He held up a hand with badly misshapen fingers. "I's 88 years old, now, you know." He smiled a toothless grin. His voice changed to a whisper. "But I might tell you a little about High John the Conqueror."

Ben leaned back on his elbows. This is what he had been hoping for. Uncle Minus only told Br'er Rabbit stories to the children. After the young ones went to bed, he told John the Conqueror stories to the grown-ups. Ben was finally getting to hear one.

Uncle Minus placed a gnarled hand on Ben's shoulder. "'Cause you see, John liked to tell stories, you understand. Kinda like me." Uncle Minus chuckled. "He liked to sometimes stretch the truth, you might say. Now Ol' Massa didn't like this, and he'd threaten John with a whipping if he kept telling lies.

"Well one day, a couple of thieves had broken into Ol' Massa's potato patch, and they was running off with a big sack of potatoes. They was coming upon the graveyard near Ol' Massa's house, and one of them said, 'Let's stop in here and divide these potatoes up between the two of us.' So they climbed up over the fence and jumped into the graveyard. But as one of them jumped, two of the potatoes fell out of the sack by the fence. They decided to go back later and get those two. They went a little further and stopped by a tree and opened up the sack and started dividing them up. 'I'll take this one, you can take that one. I'll take this one, you can take that one....'

"Well, about that time, John was heading back from the fields to Massa's house. As he was passing by the graveyard, he heard a voice saying, 'I'll take this one, you can take that one. I'll take this one, you can take that one....'

"John thought to hisself, 'That's God and the Devil in the graveyard, dividing up souls!' John got scared and ran up to the massa's house real quick.

"'Massa, Massa! The Lord and the Devil are in the graveyard, dividing up souls! I heard them with my own ears!'

"Massa said, 'Now, John, don't be lying to me again. Are you sure you heard that?'

"'Yes, Massa. Sure as you're born, that's what I heard. I heard a voice in the graveyard saying, 'I'll take this one, you can take that one.'

"Massa walked with John up to the graveyard, and they stood by the fence and listened. Sure enough, they heard a voice saying, 'I'll take this one, you can take that one. I'll take this one, you can take that one....'

"Well Ol' Massa just *knew* he'd been a good massa, so he folded his hands in prayer, and he stood there waiting for the rapture.

"Then the voice said, 'I'll take these last two, and you can take those two over there by the fence!'

"Phewww!! Phewww!! You never seen two people move so fast! Ol' Massa high-tailed it out of there going south, and John took off going north like a streak of lightning. John never saw nor heard from

Ol' Massa again."

Uncle Minus held up a crooked finger.

Everyone joined in for the last line: "And THAT'S how John got his freedom!" Almost everyone had heard the same story many times before.

People were still laughing and talking when they suddenly noticed a stranger standing in the open doorway.

★

Chapter 2

GO DOWN, MOSES

The room was quiet as a stooped, elderly woman stood looking into the room. Big Mama stood and faced her. "My name's Hannah. Come in and sit down."

Several people rose and opened the circle to make room. "Thank you. People call me Moses," the stranger said.

Big Joe's eyes narrowed. "Funny name for a woman. You don't talk like you're from around here. Where you from?"

The woman held his gaze. "I's born a slave in Maryland. Now I'm working for the Union Army down in Beaufort."

"First they tells me the Union Army has black soldiers in it, and now you're telling me they hiring women?" Big Joe said. "What're you here for?"

Moses removed one of her many shawls. "I's here to ask some questions."

Big Joe looked at her out of the corner of his eye. "What you wanna know?"

"I needs to know whose plantation this is."

Brother James looked skeptical. "Why you needing to know that?"

"Like I said, I'm working with the Union Army down in Beaufort. We're gonna try to help you folk."

Brother James and Uncle Minus locked eyes for several seconds. Another half minute went by without anyone speaking. Finally, Uncle Minus whispered. "This is Massa Lowndes' plantation."

"Lowndes," Moses repeated, nodding her head slowly. "I's hoping that's where I was. And who lives just downriver?"

"That'd be Massa Paul," said Sam. "Massa James Paul."

Big Joe folded his arms across his chest. "I don't like this."

"Take it easy, Big Joe," Uncle Minus said.

Moses pointed the other way. "And who's next upriver?"

Sam spoke again. "Massa Smith."

Once again, Moses repeated the name. "Smith."

Uncle Minus interrupted. "Colonel Heyward's plantation is across the river just beyond the ferry."

Moses turned quickly to Uncle Minus. "*Colonel* Heyward?"

"A Rebel colonel," Uncle Minus explained.

Moses looked pleased. The questioning continued for several minutes until she was asking about people and places that were too far away for them to know.

"One more thing," she said. "I needs to know if any of you seen any Rebel soldiers in these parts."

Ben glanced at Will but said nothing.

Everyone was quiet for several seconds. Brother James finally broke the silence. "Other than Colonel Heyward, I ain't seen nobody."

Big Joe laughed. "What if we have? Most of the massas along these parts gots family members fighting in this here war. We're broke out with Rebels down here, sister."

"Of course, Joshua is a soldier," Sam said. "He's Massa Lowndes' son. He left a while back, and nobody's heard from him since."

Brother James held up a finger. "Just what are you hoping to find out about these Rebel soldiers?"

"Don't know yet," Moses said. "I just know they's

gonna try and keep us from winning this war."

More silence. Moses looked around the circle until her eyes came to rest on Uncle Minus. "Now, can anybody here point me to the quarters at the Smith plantation?"

Uncle Minus started to rise. Ben quickly ran over to help him stand. Other people also rose, including Moses. "Be ready," she whispered. "It won't be long before freedom'll be here at your doorstep." The fire crackled, and the shadows played on people's faces. She began singing:

> *When Israel was in Egypt's land*
> *Let my people go!*
> *Oppressed so hard they could not stand*

The whole cabin sang the response:

> *Let my people go!*

Moses sang again:

> *Go down, Moses*
> *Way down in Egypt's land*
> *Tell Ol' Pharaoh*

And the cabin answered:

> *Let my people go!*

Silence hung in the air for several moments. Moses turned to leave, and Uncle Minus followed. Ben stood watching them, wondering if he had missed a chance to help everyone escape.

Milly was running late. Water sloshed out of her bucket as she stumbled through the doorway into the kitchen. She blew on the glowing coals before pouring water in the pan to heat.

Sophie came through the door like a hurricane, hiking up her long homespun dress. "Girl, ain't you got that coffee ready, yet? You gonna get us both in trouble!"

"Sorry, Miss Sophie." Milly stirred the coals, glancing at Sophie out of the corner of her eye. *Why don't it heat faster?* She dumped out some dried sweet potato pieces into the coffee mill and started grinding.

Sophie was already kneading biscuit dough. "They'll put you back in the fields if you don't watch out."

Sophie's years of kitchen experience helped get breakfast on the table just in time to hear Ol' Massa's daughters coming toward the dining room.

"Ouch! Give it back!"

"No. It's mine."

Two teenage girls entered the dining room. The older one was triumphantly tying a ribbon into her auburn hair as Mistress Lowndes walked in.

"What seems to be the problem this morning, girls?"

"Nothing, Mother." Susan finished tying the ribbon, and Mariah sat frowning at the table, putting her chin in her hands.

"Mariah, please take your elbows off the table," Mistress said.

Sophie carried the last serving bowl to the table as Milly placed the basket of biscuits on the sideboard. Massa Lowndes, cane in hand, limped into the room, and the family was seated.

Massa Lowndes cleared his throat and bowed his head. "Lord, make us truly thankful for the food we are about to receive. Amen."

Milly began filling coffee cups. Susan covered hers with her hand. "I don't want any of that nasty potato coffee. I'll wait till this dreadful war is over so we can buy the real thing again."

Mariah sighed. "Who knows when that'll be?"

Mistress shot a disapproving look. "Girls...."

Milly had just filled the last coffee cup. Sophie had finished serving and gone back in the kitchen to start cleaning.

Susan spooned some grits onto her plate. "Daddy,

didn't you say the Yankees had colored soldiers down in Beaufort?"

"Oh, what a mess!" Mistress said. She had spilled coffee on the tablecloth and tried to soak it up with her napkin.

Milly rushed around the table with a rag. "I'll get it, Mistress." After cleaning up the spill, she got the coffee pot and topped off Mistress Lowndes' cup, listening carefully to the conversation.

Massa Lowndes spread some butter on his biscuit. "Yes, I hear the Yankees are building up troops down in Beaufort."

Susan giggled. "I don't know what they have planned, but if they try something, they'll get a surprise from our boys up here." Milly knew Susan had her eye on George, one of the neighbors who had joined up.

Mistress picked up her napkin. "Susan, I don't want to ever hear you laughing about this war while your brother is off fighting!"

Susan leaned over the table toward her father. "Well, isn't it true, Daddy? Weren't you talking to Colonel Heyward a few days ago? If they come up in these parts, they'll get blown to pieces, won't they?"

Massa Lowndes held the breadbasket up in the air. "Milly, there were only five biscuits in here again this morning. Bring some more."

"Yes, Massa." Milly hurried out to the kitchen.

Sophie put her hands on her hips and faced Milly. "Bread already gone?"

Milly filled the basket. She quickly brought it back and offered the biscuits to Massa Lowndes.

Mistress was speaking. "I just heard news from the Paul plantation. Annette's sick with the intermittent fever. James is worried about her, and now he's afraid the baby's going to get sick."

Massa finished off his coffee. "Has the child had fever?"

"I don't think so, but he's still worried," said Mistress. "Dr. Baker's been out there twice."

Susan turned to face Milly. "Oh—Milly, I need you to hem my blue dress. I'll be wearing it the weekend after next when we go to the Rosehill Plantation."

Milly nodded. "Yes, Miss Susan."

Mariah carefully folded her napkin and put it on the table. "Mother, can't I go for just a little while?"

"I'm sorry, Mariah, but you know it's only for girls sixteen and over. They aren't going to make an exception for a thirteen-year-old."

Susan gloated. Her sixteenth birthday was on Saturday, and she had been looking forward to the gathering.

Milly filled Massa's cup and started toward the kitchen. The day had just begun, and trouble was already in the making.

Ben dropped the rice seeds into the shallow trench and covered it with his bare foot. Moving on to the next trench, he repeated the monotonous process—drop and cover. It wasn't fun, but it beat hoeing, which would start soon enough. Sweat dripped into his eyes. Just as he thought about breaking his rhythm to wipe his forehead, he heard Ol' Man Pipkin's footsteps behind him.

"Keep up the pace, now. Don't slow down!"

Ol' Man Pipkin always had his whip in hand, and he wasn't afraid to use it.

Ben didn't have to see him to know that his nose was turned upwards like he had just come across something rotten. Will called it Ol' Man Pipkin's "just-smelled-a-skunk look." A fleeting smile crossed Ben's face as he thought of Will's description.

Ben kept working. Drop and cover, drop and cover. His mouth felt like cotton.

More sweat dripped and his eyes stung.

Ol' Man Pipkin's voice was further off now. "Boy, pick it up or I'll take you over there and whip you good. You hear me?"

Drop and cover, drop and cover.

Ol' Man Pipkin hollered, "Water boys—get moving!"

Ben stood up straight and stretched backwards. He heard quick footsteps behind him, turned, and saw Thomas with the water bucket.

"Thanks, Thomas." Ben took the tin cup and dipped it into the water.

Thomas stood in his knee-length sackcloth shirt, his bare feet blending into the soil. "Sun's almost up above, ain't it, Ben?"

Ben looked up. "Uh huh. It's getting near meal time." The field hands got a short break at midday and then came back and worked until sunset. "Thomas, move fast before Ol' Man Pipkin gets you."

Thomas quickly moved to the other hands.

Before long, they heard Ol' Man Pipkin yelling, "Back to work!"

As Ben got back into the rhythm of the sowing, his mind wandered. In front of him, Big Joe was sowing seeds, with the same movements and rhythm as Ben. Big Joe's back had linear scars running in every direction—a testament to the damage of Ol' Man Pipkin's whip.

Big Mama had told Ben that Big Joe had tried to run off several times. Ben remembered the last time and wondered how far Big Joe had gotten. Ben liked the idea of running away. He smiled as he remembered the story Uncle Minus had told about John the Conqueror getting his freedom.

Ben also thought about the stories of the black soldiers down in Beaufort. If the rumors were true about Lincoln setting the slaves free, maybe Ben could join up. However, the Union Army might not let a thirteen-year-old fight, even if he did manage to escape.

Maybe Ben should go north instead of south to Beaufort. Someone had once said there was a way to go north by following the stars at night. If he got far enough, he would be free. Ben immediately felt guilty as he thought about his mother, sister, and brother. Would he escape alone and leave them behind as slaves?

Ben heard Ol' Man Pipkin's footsteps behind him. Drop and cover, drop and cover. Ben stared at Big Joe's scarred back and made a decision: He would talk to Big Joe alone.

★

Chapter 3

GOURDS AND GATORS

It had been a full day's work in the hot sun, and Ben was anxious to get the evening chores done. He grabbed the pitchfork and looked at Thomas. "Climb up there and get some hay."

Thomas scrambled into the hayloft and tossed hay down to feed the cows and mules. They quickly spread it around and secured the animals.

Outside the barn, they fed the pigs and chickens. A litter of piglets had recently been born. Most were mottled, but two were solid in color—one black and one white. They were the most playful. After they had eaten their fill, the two piglets rolled in the mud. Then the white one butted up against the black one, pushing it forward. The black one ran away, and the white piglet chased after it. They ran in circles around the pigpen. Thomas pointed and giggled.

As the boys left the barnyard, the stars were coming out. The moon was on the horizon—almost full.

Ben saw Big Joe working in the garden outside the quarters. Massa Lowndes let the slaves tend small gardens of their own so they could have some extra vegetables, but that work had to come after plantation work. This meant they were working in their gardens well into the night.

"Go on back, Thomas," said Ben. "Tell Big Mama I'll be there in a little while. I got something else to do."

"What is it?"

"Don't you worry. Go on, now."

Looking disappointed, Thomas headed off for the cabin.

Ben walked toward the garden where Big Joe was digging.

"Big Joe?"

"Whatcha need?"

"I's wanting to talk to you."

Big Joe slowly stood up. Ben craned his neck, looking upwards at the man's face. There was a reason everyone called him Big Joe. He towered over most of the people on the plantation, and his muscular trunk formed a hulking mass many wouldn't want to reckon with.

"Go on," said Big Joe.

"I wanna run away."

Big Joe laughed, picked up a hoe, and stabbed at a weed. "So you want your back to look like mine?"

"I just wanna be free."

Big Joe stared at Ben. "I ain't free."

"So you ain't gonna ever try to run again?"

"I didn't say that." Big Joe stabbed at another weed.

Ben was getting impatient. "Am I old enough to join the Union Army if I made it down to Beaufort?"

Big Joe's mouth became rigid. "Boy, I don't wanna hear that talk. You listen to me—white folk are the same all over. You can't trust any of 'em, no matter what side they on. No matter who wins this war, we'll just belong to the winner."

"How do you know that, Big Joe?"

"That's the way it's always been, son. That's the way it was for my folk and their folk before 'em. And that's the way it'll be for my young'uns and their young'uns. We don't even get to see our babies grow up." Big Joe turned his face away from Ben.

Ben felt a twinge of guilt as he thought about his

mother. Here he was trying to plan an escape, and he'd be leaving her behind. Then he remembered the Rebel soldiers and the visit by the strange woman. "What about Moses? She ain't white."

"But white people are using her. She'll find out one of these days."

"What do you mean?"

"Let me tell you something, boy. You'll hear all sorts of talk. You'll hear people say that the Union Army is Lincoln's Army, and they're out to set the slaves free. But them soldiers—it don't matter which side they're on—they ain't on your side. Them Union soldiers'll turn you back over to the slave master as quick as the Rebels will. I know."

"How you know?"

Big Joe sighed. "You remember Pompey?"

Ben nodded. Pompey had been sold from the plantation about a year ago.

Big Joe leaned on his hoe. "Pompey was always talking about joining up with the Union Army. The Union Army was our only hope, he always said. They's gonna come south and set all the slaves free. One day, Pompey finally run away. He was gone for three weeks, and I thought for sure he'd got his freedom. Then he run into some Union soldiers and asked to join up, but they just laughed. They brought him back to Massa Lowndes—got a nice reward for their troubles. You know the rest. Massa Lowndes turned around and sold him. So, Ben, I'm sure Moses'll find out one of these days. They just using her."

"Big Joe, how you know where to go when you run away?"

"It ain't easy, boy. They send the hounds out after you. You have to leave when you ain't gonna be missed for the longest amount of time. That way you get a head start. Travel by night and hide by day. You go north."

26

"Which way is north?"

Big Joe pointed overhead. The stars were easily visible. "Look up there. See them stars that make the shape of a drinking gourd?"

Ben nodded.

"The ones on the front end of the gourd always point toward the North Star. The North Star never moves. It's a long walk to Canaan Land, though. I hear there's a place called Ohio in the north. If you make it there, people'll help you get to Canaan Land."

"Canaan Land is further north?" Ben asked.

"Canaan Land is Canada, boy. Them people won't turn you back over to the slave master. If you make it there, you's free."

"Is that where you wanna go, Big Joe?"

"Every time I've run, I've headed that way. If I ever get the chance, I'll try again."

"Moses asked about Rebel soldiers. Have you seen any around?"

Big Joe nodded. "A few. Ain't telling her about it, though. They're just patrolling the river, walking the banks."

"Why not tell her about it? It won't hurt nothing, would it?"

Big Joe laughed. "Nothing but my back. If Massa Lowndes finds out I was talking to his enemy, I'd get a whipping for sure. Maybe even sold."

"Big Joe?"

"Ben, you need to get in there and help Big Mama." Big Joe stooped down and picked up his tools.

Before going to bed that night, Ben stared at the drinking gourd in the night sky. John the Conqueror had gone north for his freedom. Big Joe had also said freedom was in the north. Under the warmth of his blanket, Ben dreamed. He was running through the swampy dark woods. Then the soil began pulling his feet downward like quicksand. He had to pull each foot up out of the muddy morass until he could no longer move forward. Hounds bayed in the distance, their barking growing louder and louder. The stars above him were moving in circles. He didn't know which way to run. Just as the hounds reached him, Ben awoke in a cold sweat.

Mistress Lowndes kissed Mariah's forehead. "We're off to Rosehill." She lifted Mariah's chin. "Now don't look so dejected. Your time will come." She kissed her again.

Milly helped Susan and Mistress Lowndes climb into the carriage. Susan had a slight smirk on her face and slowly fanned herself. Her blue dress shimmered in the evening sunlight.

Sam put the overnight bags into the carriage and took his seat up front. Massa Lowndes climbed in next to his wife. "Ready, Sam."

Sam shook the reigns and the horses took off.

Susan looked backwards where Mariah and Milly were standing. "See you tomorrow, Mariah!"

Mariah stood looking at her shoes and didn't speak. The carriage left a trail of dust.

Ben watched from behind a large magnolia tree. The field hands had been let off early this evening. Someone was already tuning a fiddle, but Ben had other plans. He headed back toward the cabin to grab something to eat.

Big Mama's sixth sense took over. "Where you headed, Ben?"

"Just gonna take a walk down by the river."

"You ain't gonna stay around for the music and food?"

"I'll be back later."

Long pause. Ben hated those long pauses. When he was younger, a long pause usually meant Big

Mama wouldn't let him do something he wanted to do.

"Ben, you watch out for them gators and cotton-mouths. They're all over the place. You hear?"

"Yes'm."

"And you be back before dark."

"Yes'm."

As he left, he saw Uncle Minus buck dancing to the fiddle music. Uncle Minus could have difficulty walking from one cabin to another in the morning, but when the fiddle or banjo music started up, he lost thirty years.

Ben headed to the big magnolia tree slightly downhill from the slave quarters.

Will was already waiting. "Big Mama give you trouble?" he said.

Ben shrugged. "Not much."

They crossed the rice paddies and waded through the high grasses downward toward the river. The mosquitoes swarmed, and the boys slapped at their arms and legs. The sun was low on the horizon directly in front of them. They turned and trudged along the riverbank.

Ben stopped and looked around. "I thought it was somewhere around here, but I'm not seeing the place where I hid." He resumed walking, with Will following. Ben's heart pounded. He half expected to encounter the soldiers again.

Way up ahead, something dark was floating in the river near the bank—maybe a log? As he got closer, he realized what it was. "Looks like ol' gator's out today," he said. "I won't mention this to Big Mama." Ben had seen lots of alligators before. They would often float with their eyes just above water level.

"Something's different about this gator," said Will. "Don't really look like one."

Ben squinted. "Looks smooth, don't it?" He

glanced up the riverbank and noticed the cluster of oak trees where he had hidden a week ago.

"Ain't really shaped like a gator," said Will.

"That ain't no gator," said Ben. "Wonder if that's what the soldiers was talking about?"

"Might be."

"They also said something about the mill and them other places."

Will lifted his eyebrows. "You wanna check the mill the next time we have a chance?"

Ben nodded. "Maybe next week." He drew a deep breath. "We'll worry about the one at Colonel Heyward's fence later. That's gonna be a problem since it's on the other side of the river."

The sun was setting, and colors were fading. They took one last look at the strange, dark shape floating in the water. As they headed back to the cabins, Ben thought about the white folks' big trip to the Rosehill Plantation. He knew it was Massa Kirkland's plantation, where his mother lived. Since Sam was the coachman, he would be driving the family. Sam had promised to try to find Ben's mother. On the one hand, Ben desperately wanted to hear from her. However, he also worried that Sam might return with news she had been sold again.

Sunday night meeting was already underway. Rushing down the row of cabins, Ben could hear Brother James's voice leading a song.

> *Oh Mary, don't you weep, don't you moan*
> *Oh Mary, don't you weep, don't you moan*
> *Pharaoh's army got drownded*
> *Oh Mary, don't you weep....*

Ben slipped inside and sat on the earthen floor. He used to enjoy these meetings, but lately he dreaded all the arguments. He noticed Sam wasn't back yet. Sam was probably caring for the horses after the trip from Rosehill.

After several more songs, Brother James said a prayer. The fire crackled. "Who has something to say?" he asked.

Silence. Brother James nodded toward Ben's sister. "Milly? Any news?"

"I told you all last week about the black troops down in Beaufort. Didn't hear nothing else about it this week. Found out they're pulling soldiers away from the river 'cause of the intermittent fever."

Brother James raised his eyebrows. "Thank you, Milly."

Uncle Minus cleared his throat. "If they're pulling Rebs away from the river, maybe that'll help clear the way for them Union soldiers. Moses told us to be ready. Well, I been ready. I's ready anytime to be taken outta bondage!"

"She's working for the whites," said Big Joe. "You can't trust whites, whether they be North or South. Besides that, I'm not even sure she's with the Union. The Army ain't gonna send no woman out to tell us nothing."

"Well, I think she's working for the Union," Uncle Minus said. "She's come to help us. I trust her."

"We might be able to trust her, but where will that get us?" said Big Mama. "If the massa finds out we been telling stuff to the Union Army, we'll be in a heap o' trouble."

Uncle Minus chuckled. "Then we'll just have to make sure Ol' Massa don't find out."

Brother James raised a finger. "We gots to beware of false prophets. Sometimes a ravenous wolf comes in sheep's clothing! This woman is different. She has a strange way of talking. I think she's a conjure woman. She could be dangerous!"

Everyone started talking at once, and it was several minutes before the uproar subsided. Brother James realized that not everyone agreed with him, but he closed by saying, "I'm just telling you to be careful!" Then he led the group singing:

Tell me who's that writing,
John the Revelator
Tell me who's that writing,
John the Revelator....

Ben noticed Sam had slipped into the circle during the meeting. As they walked out, Ben caught up with him. "Sam, did you see Mama?"

"Sure did, Ben," said Sam, pulling a small piece of cloth from his pocket. Ben recognized the pattern. His mother had worn a dress made of that cloth the day she left in Massa Kirkland's carriage. Ben tried to keep those memories out of his mind. It was one thing to think about those things when he was alone, but he hated doing it when other people were around.

Sam unfolded the cloth and held it up for Ben to see. "She made this handkerchief for you."

As he felt the familiar stinging in his eyes, Ben reached out, taking the handkerchief. He managed to mumble a thanks as he turned and walked away.

★

Chapter 4

RUNAWAYS

Milly's arms felt like rubber. She had been scrubbing the kitchen floor since breakfast. The part by the stove had completely dried, and Sophie was already baking bread.

Milly heard shouts outside and then a big commotion inside the House. She wiped her hands on a rag as she ran across the passageway from the kitchen to the Big House. Sophie followed.

Mistress met them at the entrance. "Milly, you and Sophie get some tea ready. We have guests coming up the road!"

Milly got fresh water while Sophie prepared the teapot and gingerbread. "Wonder who this is, coming in the middle of the day like this?" Sophie muttered to herself. "Probably nothing but bad news. Ain't nobody bringing good news around here no more."

After the tea was brewed, Milly wheeled a serving cart out to the veranda. Massa Lowndes and Massa Smith were seated at the table, visiting. A cool breeze wafted in from the river as Milly spread a tablecloth.

Massa Smith leaned toward Massa Lowndes. "Oliver, I know Colonel Heyward lost two last week. I also heard three escaped from Edward's place last Friday. Then I talked to Walter Kirkland a couple of days ago. He said five ran off from his place last week. I tell you, I don't like this. It makes me uncomfortable."

Milly placed the plates and spoons on the table. Massa Lowndes leaned his cane against the wall. "I guess they gave us fair warning. They told us at the end of March we should move our Negroes inland. That's difficult to do during planting season, though."

Milly offered the tray to Massa Smith. He took a cup and saucer. "Colonel Heyward didn't pull his Negroes in at all," he said, as Milly filled his cup with tea. "No one else can do the work, especially with this fever going around. Is it true they have some sort of resistance to the fever that white people don't have?"

"That's what I hear," said Massa Lowndes, taking a cup and saucer. "Do they know where the escaped slaves are going?"

"Apparently, they're going south to Beaufort to join up. That's one of the reasons they sent out the warning. People are slipping onto the plantations to recruit slaves for the regiment."

Milly filled Massa Lowndes' cup, and he nodded to dismiss her. She left the teapot and bread tray and returned to the kitchen. Milly found Sophie alone, standing at the table, cutting up vegetables. Milly whispered, "Miss Sophie, Massa Smith's here. He's telling Massa Lowndes about some people who've run off."

"Girl, don't you be messing around with that business. You'll just be inviting trouble. Now bring some more water for this stew."

Milly hauled the water bucket outside. Sophie could be frustrating. She was always afraid of getting in trouble. She never went to prayer meeting because she was sure all those people would bring bad luck someday.

Sometimes Milly didn't talk to Sophie about the things she heard in the Big House, but this was different. Milly couldn't wait to tell the others. She had several days to go before prayer meeting, but she would try to find Ben tonight and tell him. He would understand how important it was.

Milly returned with the water, and Sophie added it to the vegetables. Sophie placed the pot over the fire and then turned to face Milly. "Who was it that slipped off?" Sophie whispered.

Milly stared at Sophie. "He didn't give no names. There was some at Colonel Heyward's place, some at Massa Kirkland's, and more from Massa Manigault's."

Sophie stirred the stew. Milly might have imagined it, but she thought she saw a hint of a smile on Miss Sophie's face.

On Saturday afternoon, Ben stood leaning against the big magnolia, waiting for Will. His mind wandered. Ever since Milly had told Ben about the people who had run off, he couldn't stop thinking about them. He wanted to ask Milly more questions, but they hadn't had much time to talk. Ben was especially interested in the ones who had escaped from Massa Kirkland's plantation—the place where his mother lived. He wondered if his mother had slipped away. He even hoped late at night that she might come into his cabin and take him away with her.

"You beat me!" Will waved, as he approached Ben.

Ben smiled. "First time for everything."

Ben had been to the rice mill only once. A couple of years ago, the overseer had told him to carry a sack there.

The late afternoon sun was in front of Ben and Will as they searched for the path to the mill. They had their fishing lines and poles in case someone saw them. Ol' Man Pipkin might be suspicious since slaves had been escaping from other plantations.

The tall grasses bent in the breeze. Ben and Will stopped.

"I know it's gotta be here somewhere," said Ben.

Will squinted into the sun. "If we head toward the sun, we'll find the river."

Ben turned around and looked back. "When we left the quarters, maybe we should have gone at an angle towards the Big House." He pointed diagonally to their right. "Let's go that way."

They continued trudging through the tall grasses, the sun now slightly to their left. The ground was getting softer. Their breathing became heavier as they picked up the pace.

Hearing a noise up ahead, Ben stopped and grabbed Will's arm. They stooped as low as they could. Something was rustling in the grasses, but they couldn't see anybody or hear any voices. They looked around. There were no trees nearby—no place to hide. The rustling continued for a few more seconds. Then a marsh rabbit darted in front of Ben, running a zigzag trail through the swamp. Ben let out a breath as Will stumbled forward several feet, laughing.

"Here it is!" Will said, pointing toward the river.

Ben caught up with Will and followed his gaze. The path to the mill lay in front of them. The rest of the way was easier, with the mill finally coming into view.

"Which way do we go?" Will asked.

Ben stopped. "I'm not sure. I can't remember exactly what the soldier said."

Will wiped his forehead with his sleeve. "Let's start by walking along the riverbank. That's how we found the other one."

They waded through the grasses up and down the riverbank in front of the mill, but they didn't see anything unusual in the water.

"The sun's getting low," said Ben. "Let's try upstream a little further."

They continued to trudge through the high grasses but saw nothing in the water.

"You sure it was the mill?" Will asked.

Ben glared. "I'm sure he said the mill."

"Maybe they haven't planted one here yet," said Will, shrugging. "Or maybe we're looking in the wrong place."

Ben stopped walking. "Let's head back down-stream."

When they reached the mill, the sun was setting, and it was getting difficult to see. They didn't have a lot of time on these Saturday evenings after coming in from the fields.

Will put his hand on Ben's shoulder. "We need to be getting back to the quarters."

I know that, thought Ben. He also knew that if Ol' Man Pipkin caught them outside at night, they'd be whipped. Ben's heart was pounding. "Let's just go a little further."

Something was up ahead—something dark in the water. Maybe it really was a gator this time. As Ben got closer, he realized it was indeed the same strange shape he had seen in the river where the soldiers had been.

"There it is," Ben said, pointing to the river.

"Uh huh," said Will. "That ain't no gator."

Ben stared. "You can see this one better. Both ends are pointed."

They stayed a few more minutes, then turned around and headed back to the mill. They found the path and ran back toward home, using the light from the rising moon to guide them. When the Big House loomed up ahead, they took off through the tall grasses toward the quarters.

"Good night," said Will, as he went toward his cabin.

As Ben opened the door of the shed, a deep voice

startled him. "Big Mama's worried about you. I thought you was gone for sure."

Ben looked behind him and saw Big Joe. "Naw. Just late getting back is all."

Big Joe looked at his line and pole. "Catch anything?"

"Naw."

"You ain't been catching much lately. What you been doing all evening?"

Ben looked down at the ground and remained silent.

"Planning something?"

More silence.

"You don't have to say nothing. Just remember— this is a hard time to run. They be expecting it now. They's watching us close."

✦

Chapter 5

DANGER AT DUSK

As **Ben walked down** the long row of log cabins, Uncle Minus came out of his door. For once, Ben wasn't late to prayer meeting. Uncle Minus stood bent over, leaning on his handmade cane, and looked up at Ben. "Going to prayer meeting?"

"Yes, sir. Want a hand?" Uncle Minus used his cane when nobody else was around, but he preferred to hold onto a person.

Uncle Minus took Ben's arm and continued walking. "Should be a good meeting. Guess they'll be talking about the folks that run off from them plantations. They giving Ol' Massa the slip just like Br'er Rabbit does." Uncle Minus chuckled.

"I saw a marsh rabbit yesterday, Uncle Minus."

"Did you now? Where was he?"

"Near the footpath to the mill."

"I ain't seen one of them in a while," said Uncle Minus. "Course, I ain't been out and about like I used to be. Marsh rabbits like to stay close to the water."

They reached the last cabin, and Ben let his old friend enter first. As Brother James was adding a log to the fire, Ben helped Uncle Minus sit down. People kept streaming in, including Big Mama, Will, and Milly. They sat down in a circle. Big Joe sauntered in and sat just outside it, locking eyes with Ben for a few seconds.

Brother James started the first song:
> *My God is a rock in a weary land,*
> *Weary land, in a weary land*
> *My God is a rock in a weary land*
> *Shelter in a time of storm....*

After several songs, the discussion began. Brother James called on Milly to relate the news from the Big House about the slaves who slipped off from neighboring plantations.

After her summary, Ben looked closely at Milly. "You say five ran off from Massa Kirkland's plantation?"

"Yes, five."

"Did he say who they were?" Ben asked, thinking of his mother.

"No. Massa Smith said people been sneaking onto the plantations to recruit soldiers. The ones who left are going to Beaufort to fight in the colored regiment."

Ben looked disappointed. "So the ones who ran off were all men?"

"He didn't say," said Milly.

Big Joe cleared his throat. "They're gonna regret running south. The Union Army ain't gonna treat 'em no better than the Rebels. They'll probably just turn 'em back over to the slave owners when they get down there."

"They haven't yet," said Sam. "Some of the people have been gone since last week. That's long enough to get to Beaufort and get into uniform."

Big Joe laughed. "Go on down there, then. Your back will start looking like mine pretty soon."

Uncle Minus raised a hand. "I don't know what they got in mind down in Beaufort, but anything that hinders folk who are causing problems for us can't be all bad. My enemy's enemy just *might* be my friend." Uncle Minus paused for a moment and glanced at Ben. "Now, if you folks is done with all this bickering, I thought you might like to hear what High John's been up to lately."

Several people chuckled. With one stroke, Uncle Minus had changed the mood in the cabin.

Uncle Minus began. "There was a time when Ol' Massa was being especially mean to High John, and John was getting tired of it. So John and his pal Joe rigged up a plan where they hid a whole bunch of food high in a big sycamore tree.

"Next time Ol' Massa got to fussing and complaining about how John was doing things, John said to Ol' Massa, 'I'm tired of the way you been treating me. You work me from before daylight to after dark. You don't hardly feed me. I believe from now on, I'll just go to God for my food!'

"Ol' Massa looked at John and said, 'Now John, God ain't the one feeding you. I am. So if you don't do what you're supposed to do, you'll go hungry.'

"John walked over and stood under the sycamore tree. Now Joe had already climbed up in the tree earlier and was hiding up where Ol' Massa couldn't see him. John fell down on his knees and hollered, 'Oh Lord my God, have mercy on your humble servant. If it be your will, please send me down a sack of flour.' Down came a sack of flour. John continued. 'And if it be thy holy and righteous will, dear Lord, please send your humble servant a side of meat, some sugar, a can of lard, and some rice.' Down came everything he asked for.

"Ol' Massa looked like he'd seen a ghost. His eyes were popping out. John got up from his knees and looked at Ol' Massa. 'You know something, Massa?' he said. 'I believe I'm gonna get back down on my knees and ask the Lord to destroy all these wicked folks here with a bolt of lightning! In fact, I believe I'll ask him to destroy the world!'

"Ol' Massa hollered, 'No, John, no, don't do that! I'll make you a deal. If you don't do that, I'll give you your freedom and forty acres and a thousand dollars.' So John was a wealthy man after that. And John never saw nor heard from Ol' Massa again!"

Uncle Minus held up a crooked finger, and everyone, including Ben, joined in for the last line: "And THAT'S how John got his freedom!" Uncle Minus finished with a smile and wave of his hand, and everyone laughed.

Then Brother James led a song:
> One of these days, my sister
> One of these days, my sister
> One of these days
> When the Lord call me home....

As Ben helped Uncle Minus stand at the end of the meeting, he noticed a commotion at the door of the cabin. Ben glanced over and saw Moses standing at the entrance.

Sam, who was next to Moses, called for everyone to be quiet. "Moses has something to ask us before we leave," he said.

She adjusted her shawl. "I still need to know more about them Rebel soldiers. Y'all seen anything suspicious in the river in these parts?"

Ben glanced at Will. Will opened his mouth as if he was about to say something but then stopped. After a few moments, Ben turned his attention back to Moses.

One by one, Moses looked at each person. Other than a few people whispering and the fire crackling, there was only silence in the cabin. Ben felt uncomfortable as she gazed into his eyes.

"Ain't seen no Rebel soldiers at all?" she said.

Milly's voice broke the silence. "I haven't seen anything in the river or any Rebel soldiers. I work in the Big House. I can tell you what I've heard there."

Moses nodded.

Milly continued. "Several slaves have run off from plantations nearby in the last week or two.

Colonel Heyward lost two, Massa Manigault lost three, and Massa Kirkland lost five."

"I know about that," Moses said. "Did they say anything else?"

"They said the slaves were going down to Beaufort to join the colored regiment."

Moses was silent and her face became rigid for a moment. She looked up at everyone again. "Anybody here wanting to fight for the Union Army?"

Sam raised a finger. "I've been studying on it."

Moses took him by the arm. "I'll talk to you afterwards." She turned to the group in the cabin again. "I'll be back. I know you folks gather on Sunday nights. I'll try to come on a Sunday if I can. Keep an eye out. I need to know if anyone sees any Rebel soldiers in these parts and if you find anything unusual in the river." She led Sam out, and Ben was left standing in the cabin next to Uncle Minus.

Ben lay on his pallet, staring at the ceiling. His wandering thoughts kept him from falling asleep. The soldier had mentioned the edge of the plantation—something about a cypress tree. Ben had never been downriver that far before. He knew if Ol' Man Pipkin caught him snooping around there, he would be whipped. Tomorrow was Saturday, and he and Will were going to try and find the place as soon as they came in from the fields.

Ben thought about running away. If he ran to the north, maybe he could eventually come back for the rest of his family. Something about this choice bothered him. He knew he would probably never be able to return, and the rest of his family would remain slaves.

If he ran south to Beaufort and joined the Union Army, he could fight. If they won, everybody, including his family, would be free. There were problems with this choice, also. He knew they probably wouldn't take a thirteen-year-old as a soldier. There was also the story that Big Joe told about the Union Army turning slaves back over to their masters.

The thought of running away terrified Ben. He'd seen Massa Lowndes and the overseer standing outside with the hounds getting ready for the big chase. He'd also seen them bring back people who had run off. He remembered seeing Big Joe whipped after he'd been caught. Big Joe had never let out a holler or cry the whole time.

Ben looked over at Thomas as he breathed heavily on the next pallet. Ben felt under his pillow and pulled out the handkerchief that his mother had sent. He unfolded it and held it in front of his face. He couldn't see the details in the darkness, but he remembered its pattern. "Promise to remember me to the little ones!" she had said. He blotted a tear from his cheek, folded the handkerchief, and slipped it back under the pillow.

Dark clouds gathered on Saturday as Ben finished hoeing in the rice fields. It had just started to sprinkle when the horn blew and he headed for the barn with Thomas to do chores. By the time he left the shed with his line and pole, a light rain was falling. Nothing would stop him from going to the river today, though.

Will was waiting for him at the big magnolia below the slave quarters.

"Sorry I'm late," said Ben. "Had to finish up chores in the barn."

Will shrugged. "Just got here myself."

They wove through the stands of magnolias and cypress and began trudging through the sea of high grass. Before long, they saw the river in the distance.

Ben pointed ahead. "Let's head downriver. We might have to search the same way we did at the mill." As he looked overhead at the clouds, a raindrop hit him in the eye. "We won't have much daylight today."

As they waded through the grasses, the rain slacked off again. Will touched Ben on the sleeve. "Look," he said.

Up ahead on the riverbank, a large cypress stood. Just below the tree, Ben saw some movement. The boys slowed their pace but kept walking.

Ben followed Will's gaze. "What is it?"

Will stopped walking. "Soldiers, I think."

"I see 'em," said Ben. "Looks like two soldiers. Gray uniforms."

"They're talking."

"One just bent over," said Ben. "I think he's touching something on the ground."

The boys crouched in the grasses and watched. The soldiers talked a little longer and then walked downstream, carrying something in their hands.

Will stood. "Let's go see if they left anything."

"No!" Ben grabbed Will's arm and pulled him back. "Not yet. Let's give 'em a few minutes and make sure they aren't coming back."

Will looked up into the darkening sky. "We don't have much time."

"If we get caught, we won't have *any* time. Let's just wait a little longer."

After several minutes, Ben agreed to continue their trek to the riverbank. They headed for the spot where they had seen the soldiers. Every few feet they stopped and crouched, looking to make sure nobody was about.

Dusk was coming early, and the marsh had already turned into a black-and-white world. Ben knew they needed to save a little daylight for the trip back to the quarters. Big Mama was right about cottonmouths—they could be dangerous, especially if you stepped on one.

They were finally at the riverbank.

Will stopped. "What's that?"

Something was right in front of them—right on the bank.

Ben stared at it. "Is it a log?"

"Or maybe it's one of those things we're looking for, and they left it on the bank instead of in the river," Will said.

Ben crept a little closer. "Maybe we can finally get a good look at one." The rain had stopped. If those clouds would only move away from the horizon....

The "log" dove into the water with a splash and disappeared. Ben felt his heart beating in his throat as he realized that the "log" had been an alligator. As he watched the rings on the water disappear, he saw something a little further downstream.

Ben pointed at the water and looked at Will. "Let's look at that."

Will's eyes were still wide open from the encounter with the alligator. "I hope that's not another gator," he said.

They walked along the riverbank and found the familiar smooth shape floating in the water. It looked just like the other two objects Ben had seen.

Ben turned toward the cypress. "Huge tree."

Will nodded. "I think we could find this place again."

Ben glanced in the direction the soldiers had gone but saw nobody. He scanned in other directions also. So far, so good. He tried not to think about the close call with the alligator.

The way back was difficult in the dark through the wet, tall grass. The mosquitoes were swarming and buzzing in their ears. They had never stayed out this late before. As they approached the area of the

Big House, the cypress trees stood guard. The boys turned toward the quarters but heard a noise up ahead. They froze.

In the distance, they saw Ol' Man Pipkin walking away from the slave quarters, going toward the Big House. He had his whip in hand, and he stopped for a few moments, looked backwards, and then proceeded.

"What's he doing out this late?" Will whispered.

"Don't know."

"You think he knows we're gone?" Will said, his voice sounding panicky.

"I don't know, but we better get back."

Ben and Will walked toward the quarters, giving Ol' Man Pipkin a wide berth.

At the big magnolia, Will raised his hand. "See ya tomorrow, Ben."

"See ya."

Ben climbed the slope toward the cabin and placed the line and pole in the shed. Lately, he had been coming up with a lot of excuses for not catching any fish. Maybe he could slip in the cabin without Big Mama noticing.

However, as he opened the cabin door, Big Mama was standing on the other side, looking at him with her hands on her hips. "Just what do you think you're doing, staying out this late?"

Ben stared at his feet. "Sorry."

Big Mama stepped forward and shut the door behind Ben. "Ol' Man Pipkin was here."

⭐

Chapter 6

THE WHIPPING TREE

Big **Mama's brow was furrowed** into a deep V as she fretted and fussed about the cabin, mumbling under her breath. "Tried to bring him up proper. Did my best to keep him outta trouble, and look what happens."

Ben stared at her. He knew he was in deep trouble with Ol' Man Pipkin. It was painful to see that Big Mama thought it was her fault.

One of the sleeping children whimpered. Big Mama scooped him up, singing, "Hush little baby, don't you cry," as she rocked the little boy back and forth. When the child was asleep again, she placed him back in bed.

Picking up a pan of dirty water, Big Mama headed toward the door. Ben noticed the deep V on her brow had returned. He hurried to open the door for her. After dumping the water outside, she came back, mumbling under her breath again. "...just like Solomon. He runs off and don't even consider nobody else..."

Ben put his hand on her arm. "Who's Solomon?"

She stared at him out of the corner of her eye for a few seconds. Then she shook his hand off her arm and kept walking.

Ben persisted. "Who's Solomon? Someone used to be here?"

Big Mama took off her apron and threw it on the table. She sat down next to Ben. "Solomon was my older brother," she said. "Ever since I can remember, he always talked about getting away from slavery. And when he got to where he was old enough, he ran away."

"Did they catch him?"

"They sent out the hounds. They tried for weeks, but they never caught him."

"I bet you was glad he got away."

Big Mama snorted. "But that's when life got even harder for us."

"What do you mean?"

"Solomon left all of us behind—Mama, Daddy, me, my sister. Our family had been owned by Ol' Massa's family for generations. When Solomon escaped, it made Ol' Massa mad. First thing he did was sell Mama and Daddy."

"He sold 'em both?"

"He didn't sell 'em to the same massa neither. I never seen 'em again." Big Mama pulled a rag out of her dress pocket. She dabbed at her eyes.

"He kept you?" Ben's voice was shaky.

Big Mama nodded. "He kept me, sure enough. Massa'd been letting me work in the Big House for a couple of years. But I didn't work the Big House no more after that. Got put back in the fields."

"What about your sister?"

"She was already working the fields. She stayed in the fields for a while. Ol' Massa sold her about six months later."

"I didn't know…"

"This was Massa Lowndes' father," said Big Mama, sniffing. "That wasn't all he did."

"What do you mean?"

Big Mama pointed to her left cheek. "You know this here scar?"

Ben knew about the scar. Everybody knew about the scar. It was hard to miss. "He did that?"

Big Mama nodded and looked down into her lap.

She twisted her rag in her hands.

"Did he hit you or something?"

She raised the rag to her face. "He branded me." Her shoulders began to shake convulsively. Ben put his hand on her arm. Big Mama had always been the strong one. She'd always been the glue that held everyone together. He had never seen her so weak— so vulnerable.

"Wish we could all get away from here, Big Mama. I'm tired of these..."

"Ben, I don't want you to *never* run away." Big Mama's voice rose. "Every time you been gone, I been worried." A tear ran down her cheek.

"Don't you wanna be free, Big Mama? Our chance might be coming if this talk about the Union army is true."

"Course I wanna be free. But sometime it scares me thinking about it. Like when we're at Sunday meeting and that woman Moses come and ask questions. If Massa Lowndes ever catch us meeting with her, we could all get in big trouble—just like old times." Big Mama's eyes filled again with tears.

"But times have changed," Ben said.

Big Mama put her hand on Ben's. "I hope so," she said. "I hope so."

They sat together for a long time, not saying anything. Ben thought about the next day—about Ol' Man Pipkin. Ben would tell him he had gone fishing. That story made sense since he had taken his line and pole, and that's what he had told Big Mama. He'd simply stayed out too long, hoping he might catch something. He'd had bad luck fishing, that's all. Maybe Ol' Man Pipkin would buy his story.

Big Mama interrupted his thoughts. "I hope Ol' Man Pipkin don't hurt you too bad tomorrow."

"Don't worry none about me. I'll be all right."

"That's what Solomon said. And I guess he was all right. But he sure left a mess behind him."

"I'll keep that in mind."

"Just think about it, child. Think about it. That's all I ask. Before you go off and do something crazy, think about what it means to somebody else you care about." Big Mama put her arms around Ben. Her body felt familiar and friendly. She smelled like gingerbread. When he was younger and his mother was working the fields, he had always enjoyed sitting in her lap. Ben surrendered and returned her embrace.

Ol' Man Pipkin's weather-beaten face, with his just-smelled-a-skunk look, contorted even more into a nasty grimace as he grilled Ben. "I said, where were you last night, boy?"

This was the moment Ben had been dreading. Ever since Big Mama had told him about Ol' Man Pipkin, he had been rehearsing what he was going to say. Now the words wouldn't come. "I..." His tongue stuck to the roof of his mouth.

"Where, boy?" Ol' Man Pipkin raised his right hand, and the whip dangled.

Ben managed to get two words out. "Fishing, suh."

"Fishing?" Pipkin hollered. "Fishing? In the dark?"

"I...I hadn't caught anything, and I fished a little longer—thinking I might catch something."

There was a long silence—a bad silence. Ben had seen what Ol' Man Pipkin could do to people.

Pipkin glared at Ben. "You ain't too young to whip, you know."

"I'm sorry, suh."

"Get over there by that magnolia," Pipkin hollered.

Ben stared at the overseer. He couldn't believe what he was hearing. The magnolia was where the whippings took place.

"I said get over there by that tree," Pipkin hollered even louder.

Ben heard a short cry. He didn't have to look to know it had been Big Mama's voice. By now, a crowd had gathered, but Ben didn't look anyone in the eye. He walked to the magnolia.

"Turn around, boy."

Ben turned to face the tree, his back to Ol' Man Pipkin. Ben's fingers gripped the rough bark, and he lowered his head, leaning it against the trunk. He heard the whip before he felt it. It was over before he felt the stinging, the burning, the aching, and something dripping down his back. He waited for the next one.

"This boy stayed out a little too late last night," Pipkin yelled, enjoying the spectacle. "I'm giving him one lash this time. He'll get more next time. Let this be a lesson to all of you. Now get out in the fields and get to work!"

Big Mama was at Ben's side before he could turn around. "You okay?"

"I'm fine."

Ben turned and saw the crowd watching him. Will was on his right side, staring at him.

Big Mama was gently fingering Ben's back. "You wanna come to the cabin and let me clean this up?"

"No, I better get in the fields before Ol' Man Pipkin gets more upset," Ben said.

Big Mama sighed. "I'll look at it tonight." She grabbed a couple of small children by the hands and took off toward the quarters. The crowd was dispersing, most heading toward the fields to begin the day's work.

Ben picked his straw hat off the ground and started walking.

Will joined him. "Sorry, Ben."

"No matter."

"Thanks for not telling on me."

Ben glared at Will. "You didn't think I'd do that, did ya?"

Will looked around and lowered his voice. "You still gonna go up to Colonel Heyward's sometime to see what the soldiers put up there, or have you changed your mind?"

"Ain't gonna let that man stop me," Ben said. "Sure, I'm still going."

"When?"

Ben swatted at a mosquito. "How about Sunday afternoon?"

"Sounds good to me. But we got to get back earlier this time."

Chapter 7

THE CONJURE WOMAN

Mistress Lowndes fingered the material on the unfinished dress that Susan was wearing. "Sophie, the sleeves should puff out and hang to the elbow."

Sophie gathered some material together at the sleeves. "Hold the pincushion, Millie."

"Yes'm," said Milly.

Susan glanced sideways. "Mother, can't the neckline be a little lower?"

"It stays the way it is."

Susan scowled as Mistress Lowndes walked out. Sophie continued to insert pins into the dress.

"Hold still, Miss Susan, or you're gonna get stuck!"

"I'm holding as still as I can, Sophie. It's dreadfully hot today," Susan said, fanning herself.

"Okay, there's the sleeves." Sophie kneeled. "Now for the bottom. I'm putting a small piece of it up. You stand over there, Milly, and tell me if it needs adjusting."

"Looks about right, Miss Sophie."

"When will you get to my dress?" Mariah said. She was curled up on the canopy bed leafing through the pages of a book.

"We'll get to yours soon enough," said Sophie. "The gathering ain't for another three weeks. There's plenty of time."

"It's no fun anyway, having to stand here still as

a mouse," said Susan.

"Milly, you take it from here," Sophie said, standing up. "Just keep pinning it up. I gotta finish that bread in the kitchen." She walked out, and Milly took over.

Mariah put her book aside and began brushing her hair. "Who do you think will be at the party?"

Susan laughed through her nose. "Probably not any *men* since they're off fighting. I'm just going because I'm so bored sitting around here all day."

Mariah glared at Susan. "At least you got to go to Colonel Heyward's last week with Daddy."

Susan looked disappointed. "And he didn't say a word about George."

Mariah raised her voice. "Is he all you care about? What about Joshua, your own brother?"

"Of course I care about him, Mariah. It's just that nobody ever talks about George, so I have to find out things on my own. Milly, aren't you done pinning this thing up yet?"

"Almost done, Miss Susan," Milly said.

"Did Colonel Heyward say anything about the slaves that had escaped?" Mariah asked.

"Yes, he did. He never did get his slaves back, and one of them was his coachman. Colonel Heyward treated him real well. I can't imagine why he'd want to leave."

"Maybe he just wanted to be free," said Mariah.

Milly glanced at Mariah out of the corner of her eye, then continued pinning up the skirt.

"What a ridiculous notion," Susan said. "Those people wouldn't know how to live if they didn't have people telling them what to do."

Mariah rolled her eyes at Susan.

"Anyway," said Susan, "Colonel Heyward said he heard something about a colored woman who's hiding in the woods helping slaves."

Milly stuck her finger on a pin and drew back her

hand. Susan and Mariah didn't notice.

Mariah raised her eyebrows. "A free colored woman?"

Susan shrugged. "Colonel Heyward didn't know. It's just hearsay, anyway."

Milly put the last pin in the dress and stood up. "This looks nice on you, Miss Susan."

Ben's arms ached as he walked with Thomas to the barn on Saturday evening. The long weeks of hoeing had begun, and it would be another week or two before the soreness in his muscles would go away.

Thomas scrambled into the loft. "There gonna be music tonight?"

Ben spread the hay with the pitchfork. "Maybe."

The barn door opened, and Will stuck his head in. "Ben...guess who's here? That Moses woman..."

Ben stopped working. "Where?"

"Up at the last cabin."

Thomas jumped down from the loft and hollered, "Who's that?"

"Shhh!" Ben stooped down and held Thomas's hands. "Be quiet. Don't let nobody hear."

"A secret?" Thomas said.

"Yes, a secret," Ben said.

"It's real important," Will told Thomas. "If the white folks find out, we'll all get in trouble."

Thomas drew up his eyebrows. "What is it?"

Ben gave Will a meaningful look. "Let's go by my cabin first." He put the pitchfork in the shed and led Thomas toward their cabin. Will followed.

When they walked in the door, Big Mama grabbed Thomas's hand. "Bedtime," she said.

"No!" Thomas wailed.

"Quiet." Big Mama led him into the side room where the young children slept and came back removing her apron. "Have you heard who's here?"

"Moses?" Ben said.

"Uh huh. Let's go." Big Mama tied her hair up as they walked out the door.

Moses sat next to the fire in the last cabin. People were coming in two or three at a time. Ben and Will came in and sat next to each other.

"I'm missing some information," Moses said to Brother James.

"What kind of information?" he said.

"I'm still needing to know if any of you've seen any soldiers about."

By now, a crowd of people had gathered and sat in a circle around the fire. Brother James waited until people were settled before speaking. "Moses came tonight to ask us some questions." He nodded toward her.

"Anyone seen any Rebel soldiers in these parts since I was here last?" she asked. No one spoke.

Big Joe cleared his throat. "Why do you keep asking us the same thing over and over? Why don't *you* give *us* some information?"

Moses stared at Big Joe. "All right. I'll tell you something. Them Rebels are putting things in the river—things that'll blow up. They call 'em torpedoes. We're trying to find out where they are."

Ben looked at Will.

"These torpedoes—will they hurt us?" Big Joe asked.

"They'll blow up them Union gunboats when they come up the river. And if them boats can't make it up the river, they can't help you folks."

"Them Union soldiers ain't gonna help us noways," Big Joe said, putting his hands behind his head and leaning against the wall.

"I think we need to help this woman," said Sam. "She's trying to help us."

Everyone began talking at once. After a few

moments of argument, Brother James called for people's attention. "Let's discuss this with respect for one another. Sam, you got a question?"

"You say them Rebels are putting things in the river?" Sam asked.

"Torpedoes," said Moses.

"How many are there?"

"That's one thing we don't know yet. We're trying to find out..."

Moses stopped talking. Her eyes rolled upwards, her head dropped forward, and she continued to sit silently.

"Moses?" Brother James said.

She didn't respond. People began whispering. A whole minute went by. Another minute.

"You saying anything?" Will whispered in Ben's ear.

"No way," Ben said.

Another minute.

"We're trying to find out how many torpedoes there are," Moses said. She had awakened from her "sleep" and answered the question as if nothing had happened. The room became quiet as everyone stared at her.

After an awkward silence, Brother James said, "Nobody got nothing else to say?"

No one spoke.

"I'll try and make it here sometime next week," Moses said. She rose and put on her shawl.

Brother James nodded. Sam rose and led her out of the cabin.

As soon as she was out of earshot, Brother James held up his hand and whispered, "And what did I say? I told you she was a conjure woman! She's come to lead us astray!"

People began talking again. A soft rain fell as Ben and Will left the cabin. "What did she call them things in the river?" said Will.

"Torpedoes, I think," said Ben.

"So they'll blow up a boat. That's pretty scary. You still ain't gonna say nothing?" said Will.

"No."

"Why not?"

Ben didn't answer right away. The truth was he wasn't sure why he wasn't telling. He now realized this was much bigger than whether he could go fishing or not. Maybe Will was right. "You think I should tell 'em—even Moses—about the torpedoes?"

Will shrugged. "What harm could it do?"

"Well, if Massa Lowndes finds out…"

"We'd get whipped."

"Or sold," Ben said. "I know what Big Joe would say."

"That's easy." Will deepened his voice. "You can't trust any of them white folks."

Ben smiled and nodded. "Big Joe would say that if we told Moses about the torpedoes, the Union Army wouldn't do nothing to help us."

Will ducked under a tree near his cabin. "Moses said we should be ready. She made it sound like something's about to happen."

"The problem is…I don't know if I trust her," Ben said.

"I know what you mean," said Will. "When her eyes rolled up in her head, that was creepy."

⭐

Chapter 8

CROSSING THE COMBAHEE

Ben opened up his pallet in the corner of the cabin and smoothed out the blanket. Tomorrow was going to be a rough day, and he needed to think. Somehow, he and Will had to cross the river and get to Colonel Heyward's place without being seen. Good thing Big Mama didn't know about this one.

He felt a pair of eyes behind him and turned around—Thomas. "Ben, lemme sleep here next to you tonight."

I don't need him talking to me all night long, thought Ben.

"Ben, can I sleep here tonight?" Thomas's mouth drooped a little at the edges.

Ben, promise to remember me to the little ones.

Ben squeezed Thomas's shoulder. "I guess you can stay."

Thomas smiled and left to get his bedding. Ben got up, slipped out the front door, and stared at the cloudless sky. He found the drinking gourd with its front two stars pointing northward. He wondered how far Big Joe had gone before he had been caught. Maybe Big Joe didn't even know.

When Uncle Minus was telling stories about High John the Conqueror, Ben realized he always pictured Big Joe. However, there was a crucial difference between High John and Big Joe. John was always tricking the master, winning, and getting his freedom. People liked John, not only because he won, but because he made them laugh. Big Joe didn't think there was any reason to smile anymore. He didn't even laugh at the stories Uncle Minus told.

"Ben, you coming to bed?"

Ben turned and saw Thomas peeking out the open door with his blanket in his arm.

"Go on, Thomas. I'll be there."

Ben stared a little longer at the stars before turning and closing the door. After they were settled, Ben pulled out the handkerchief his mother had given him and held it up.

"What's that, Ben?"

"Mama made this for me. She gave it to Sam on his last trip to the Rosehill Plantation."

"Can I touch it?"

"Sure," Ben said. "Hold it for a while."

"What was Mama like, Ben?"

"You don't remember?"

Thomas lowered his eyes. "Not much anymore."

"Well, for one thing, she was a good cook. She could take an ol' dry peck of corn and them fat meat rations they give us and make something tasty." Ben realized he was still hungry. "And when she'd smile, her whole face would smile. Her eyes would disappear and it would be like a Sunday morning when you don't have to go out in the fields and work." Thomas giggled and Ben continued. "That handkerchief in your hand—she used to wear a dress made out of that cloth. And Thomas, she'd always hold you at night and sing you to sleep."

"I wish I could see her right now."

"I do too. Maybe someday we'll get to see her again. You remember her name?"

"Martha's her real name," Thomas said.

"That's right. And what do the white folks call her?"

Thomas scowled. "Rabbit."

"Uh huh. Now, we both need to get some sleep."

Thomas yawned and turned over on his side. Ben folded the handkerchief and placed it under his pillow.

Staring into the darkness, Ben imagined the stars again—the drinking gourd, pointing toward freedom. High John's up there somewhere free— in Canaan Land. And Ben was trying to get there. The stars circled overhead, no longer staying in one place. Ben was running, running through the swamp grass, running through the muck. The running got slower and more difficult. He tried lifting his feet out of the mud, but it held him like quicksand. Mosquitoes were swarming around his face, and the water bugs bit his legs. He heard the familiar hounds baying in the distance and knew he was once again trapped.

Ben awoke in a sweat with his heart and head pounding. Another nightmare.

Ben held his line and pole in one hand and stuck his head in the cabin door. "All finished with my chores."

"Just a minute, Ben." Big Mama wiped her hands on a rag and walked toward him. "Where you headed?"

"Down to the river. Fishing."

Big Mama gave Ben a sharp look. "How long you gonna be this time?"

"Don't know. I'll be back before dark."

"Make sure you are. Ol' Man Pipkin won't hold it at one lash next time. You remember what we talked about, now."

"Yes'm."

Ben took off toward the magnolia. As usual, Will was already waiting.

"Thought Brother James wasn't ever gonna stop

preaching this morning," Will said.

Ben smiled. "I didn't think he was gonna save any for next Sunday."

They trudged through the tall grasses. The blue sky and gentle breeze could have tricked them into thinking they were out for a pleasure walk, but they knew a formidable task lay ahead.

Will cleared his throat. "Got any ideas how we're gonna do this?"

Ben shrugged. "Well, I've heard about a bridge on Colonel Heyward's property. We could cross there and head up to..."

"Someone might see us. The soldiers might be watching the bridge."

Ben nodded. "I thought of that."

Will stepped over a fallen branch. "You don't know of any boats around here, do you?"

"No, but someone might see us in a boat, too."

"Depends on where we cross."

Ben sighed. "Let's just see what we find."

They reached the river, just upstream from the mill.

"Colonel Heyward's plantation is upriver from here," Ben said. "Let's keep walking and try to find a place to cross."

Will started walking upstream. "Lucky we got more time today."

The high grasses and weeds along the riverbank slowed them down.

Ben stopped once to wipe sweat from his forehead. "Ain't no boats around."

Will pointed across the river. "Is that a fence up ahead?"

"That must be Colonel Heyward's fence. Guess we made it."

"Except we're on the wrong side of the river."

Ben shaded his eyes from the afternoon sun. "How about swimming?"

"You fooling? With torpedoes in that river?"

"I gotta see what's over there."

Will had a look of disbelief on his face. "And gators? Snakes? Ben, this is stupid."

"I'll try it if you do. Course, if you're scared..."

"All right, Ben, all right."

Ben leaned his line and pole against a tree. "We'll leave our fishing things here and get 'em on the way back."

Ben examined the opposite bank. "See the corner of the fence? That's where the torpedo should be in the river. So we need to cross downstream from there."

"What if they're a little off?"

Ben smirked. "Don't worry. Just watch where you're swimming. We'll be all right."

Without any further warning, Ben jumped in the water and began swimming toward the opposite bank. Will was left on the bank, staring.

Ben was already a fourth of the way across when he turned around and looked back at Will. "You coming?"

Will hesitated, then jumped in. Ben watched as Will trudged along, awkwardly moving his arms back and forth. Ben had always been the better swimmer. He swam a few more strokes. The water was refreshing after being in the hot sun, with gnats and mosquitoes swarming around their faces. Ben and Will had been swimming in the river before, but it was always with other people—definitely when adults were around to keep an eye out for alligators and snakes. There were always the stories, usually told by the old folks, of people who had been attacked by gators or bitten by snakes. Some of them had lived and some had not.

Ben stopped swimming and looked behind. Will had dropped back farther. Ben turned forward again—he was halfway across. He scanned the riverbank. Couldn't see much—the sun was in his eyes. It was probably too hot for gators to be up on the banks right now. Which means they'd be in the water. *The water we're swimming in*, Ben thought. Ben looked back at Will's flailing arms. *Can't you go any faster? Swim. Swim harder. We need to get out of here.*

Ben felt something brush up against his leg. A fish? Or something else? He couldn't wait any longer. He ducked down and swam underwater for a while. Then he surfaced and looked around. The riverbank was just ahead; Colonel Heyward's fence was up-stream—he was coming in at a good place. Then he turned, looking behind again. Will had somehow dis-appeared. Ben scanned the water, searching down-stream, then upstream. Something dark was floating in the water upstream, directly below the corner of Colonel Heyward's fence. Ben shuddered. *The torpe-do? Or a gator?* Once they reached the riverbank, he and Will could get a better look at it. Ben searched again, upstream and downstream. *Maybe Will is swimming underwater,* he thought. *But does Will even know how to swim underwater?* Several seconds went by, but they seemed like minutes. Something upstream caught his eye. He glanced over and saw Will's head bobbing up and down in the distance. *And he's headed right for the torpedo—or gator—or whatever it is!*

Ben didn't waste any time. He aimed at a point between Will and the dark object and swam harder than he had ever done in his life. He hoped he could go fast enough against the current to stop Will in time. After several strong strokes, Ben glanced up. Will was now closer to the dark thing. Ben dropped back down in the water and swam farther upstream. He stopped again and wiped his face. Will hadn't changed direction.

"Will!" Ben yelled.

Will didn't hear him, his head now periodically

going underwater and his arms flailing, slapping at the surface. Somehow, he was still moving forward. Within seconds, he would hit the dark thing. And if that happened—well, Ben didn't even want to think about it. Ben dropped down in the water and redoubled his efforts, pulling back with his arms and kicking hard. He was almost there.

Ben's head hit something. He looked up—it was Will. Ben grabbed Will's arm and swam downstream, then toward the riverbank. Soon they were both on the bank with their sides heaving.

Will pointed upstream, breathing heavily. "I saw something up there."

Ben nodded. "Torpedo or a gator. You almost swam right into it."

Will wiped his face. "Thanks for coming to get me."

"Let's go look at it."

They walked upstream along the riverbank until they came to the spot where the dark thing floated in the water.

"Torpedo," said Will.

Ben glanced up at Colonel Heyward's fence. "Well, it's downhill from the corner of the fence, just like the soldiers said."

"I would have been upset if this one hadn't been here after all we went through."

"I'm glad you didn't swim into it."

Will looked up and down the riverbank. "Wonder if there's a boat on this side of the river?"

Ben laughed. "How did you end up going the wrong way?"

Will's voice rose. "I couldn't find you."

"I guess I was swimming underwater a lot. I'll try to swim on top more this time so you can see me. Let's try to swim side by side this time and stay together."

"Uh huh," said Will, sounding unconvinced.

Ben started walking along the bank. "Let's start downriver a piece, away from that torpedo."

Will followed, then stopped. "Ben, ain't nothing gonna get me in that water again. I nearly got killed."

Ben looked back at Will. "We *have* to get over there somehow. We're on the wrong side of the river."

Will shook his head. "I don't care."

Ben's voice rose this time. "If we don't get back to the plantation, the hounds'll come after us. You want that? Ol' Man Pipkin'll whip us both."

Will's jaw was rigid. He didn't respond.

Ben started walking again. "Sun won't be in your eyes this time. Should be easier."

Will hesitated, then continued walking.

"How about here? See that clump of cypress trees?" Ben pointed to the opposite bank. "Keep your eye on those, and we'll swim toward them. Ready?"

"I guess," Will said, sounding unconvinced.

"You first, and I'll follow," Ben said.

Will hesitated, then jumped into the Combahee River. Ben followed and pulled up alongside Will. This time, Ben spent most of his time paddling with his arms, kicking with his legs, and shouting encouragement when Will came up for air. Ben scanned the water and banks for gators, snakes, and people.

When they neared the bank, Ben thought he saw something—yes, he definitely saw it. Between him and the riverbank, a cottonmouth was swimming with its head out of the water.

Ben grabbed Will's arm. "Will—this way." Ben jerked his arm sideways. Will probably thought he was crazy. Ben chanced a glance toward the snake. It had sighted them, turned, and faced them. Ben knew they were dangerously close.

"What are you doing?" Will said, struggling against Ben's grip. "You're taking us away from the cypress trees."

"Stop," Ben said, staring at the cottonmouth. "Be still."

Will followed Ben's gaze. Just then, the snake opened its mouth and gaped at the two boys.

"Just swim backwards real slow," said Ben.

Will's voice rose. "I have enough trouble swimming forwards."

Ben grabbed Will's arm and swam away from the snake, going parallel to the riverbank. He gradually got close enough to the bank so they could climb out.

Ben went upstream a short distance to retrieve their fishing poles. When he came back, Will was sitting on the bank with his head in his hands. Ben chuckled. "Ready for another swim?"

Will smirked.

The boys' wet clothes clung to them as they trudged through the dry grasses on the riverbank. The sun was finally nearing the horizon on the other side of the water, promising a red sunset. By the time they reached the mill, they turned back through the woods heading home.

When they reached the quarters, the boys' clothes were mostly dry. Ben walked toward the shed near his cabin. "Got chores to do before Sunday night meeting. See you later?"

"Guess so." Will smiled. "You're a regular Union spy, Ben."

Ben put his hands on his hips. "I guess that depends on whether or not I give 'em the information."

★

Chapter 9

TO TELL OR NOT TO TELL

Sunday meeting was over, and people were filing out of the cabin. Ben turned to Will and said, "No need to wait for me. I'm gonna talk to Big Joe about something."

"All right," Will said. "See you later."

Ben caught up with Big Joe.

"Whatcha want?" Big Joe said.

"Can I talk to you a minute?"

"I'm listening."

Ben walked away from the crowd and lowered his voice. "You told me you always run north when you run away. How far did you get before you got caught?"

"Can't hardly say, Ben. I's gone for eight days once. So you still thinking about running, huh?"

Ben nodded. "How do you keep the hounds from tracking you?"

Big Joe's eyebrows knitted together. "I stayed in the water as much as I could. That confuses the hounds 'cause they can't get my scent."

Ben smiled. "So you're tricking 'em just like High John?"

Big Joe frowned. "High John ain't real. Never was real. High John's just wishful thinking. Just stories."

"But they're good stories. And they give people hope."

Big Joe grunted. "False hope."

"I can't stand the thought of just staying here, doing nothing."

Big Joe's jaw tightened. "It's harder to run now. They're expecting it. They're watching us close, boy."

"You still think Moses and the Union Army'll turn against us?"

Big Joe put his hand on Ben's shoulder. "Ben, I think Moses means well. But the Union Army will turn against her and the rest of us. There's no use helping any of them people. They'll cheat us in the end."

"You know anything about the people who escaped from the other plantations?"

"I don't know nothing about that. All I know is that them people are making it harder for me to run."

Ben looked around in the darkness before responding. "You gonna try and slip away again, Big Joe?" It came out as a whisper.

Big Joe shrugged and looked down at his feet. "Maybe. Maybe not. Who knows?"

The sun bore down strongly in the middle of May, and workdays were long. Another week of heavy hoeing went by. Ben spent long hours in the fields trying to decide whether to tell about the Rebel soldiers and the torpedoes. By the end of the week, he was no closer to a decision.

Ben shuffled to Sunday meeting still pondering his dilemma. Somewhere in the background, he heard, "Can't you hear me?"

Ben looked over to see Will walking behind him. "Oh...sorry...I was thinking about something."

"I asked if you had decided anything or not... about telling folks..."

Ben shook his head. "No, I still don't know."

The singing began in the last cabin. Will edged

closer to Ben. "I had to work in the orchard most of yesterday or I would have tried to talk to you. I think you should tell 'em about the soldiers."

Ben walked a little slower as they neared the cabin. "I had about decided on telling people until..."

"Until what?" Will said, as he led Ben away from the cabins to a nearby tree.

"If I tell Moses about it and Massa Lowndes finds out, then lots of us could get in trouble."

Will snorted. "So you ain't gonna tell 'cause you *might* get us in trouble," he said, his voice dripping sarcasm, "even though you've got a chance to set us all free."

"Tell 'em yourself if you want," Ben said, his voice rising.

Will didn't answer.

By the time the two boys entered Sunday meeting, the singing was drawing to a close and Brother James was beginning his prayer. The two boys slipped into the circle. After the prayer, Brother James looked around at everybody and asked his usual question, "Who has something to say?" Nobody seemed to want to start the conversation. Big Joe sat in the corner, as usual, with his arms crossed and his straw hat tilted to one side. Big Mama's face was impassive. Sam sat in the circle with his chin in his hands.

Outside, a voice broke the silence. It was a powerful, husky voice:

When Israel was in Egypt's land

The voice paused, waiting for them to respond. Uncle Minus led the response:

Let my people go!

Outside, the voice sang again:

Oppressed so hard they could not stand

And the people in the cabin replied:

Let my people go!

Moses appeared in the doorway, and sang,

71

Go down, Moses
Then the whole cabin joined her:
Way down in Egypt's land
Tell Ol' Pharaoh
Let my people go!

After a few moments of silence, Sam rose and helped Moses sit down in the circle. Brother James cleared his throat and looked at Moses out of the corner of his eye. "Moses, what brings you here tonight?"

Moses removed her shawl. "Just as always, Brother James, I'm here to see if you have anything new to tell me. Anybody seen any Rebel soldiers in these parts?" She scanned the circle of eyes one by one. Big Joe was sitting in the shadows and avoided looking at her. Nobody responded.

"Anything different in the river, then?" she said. "Nobody seen nothing in the river?"

No response.

"This is the one place I can't seem to get information," Moses continued. "I know about everyplace else. But you people ain't helping me at all." Once again, she looked around at each person. Will looked at his fingernails. When she came to Ben, her eyes lingered. Ben's heart pounded in his chest. Time passed. Surely half a minute. Maybe a minute. Finally she looked at the next person.

"You people don't seem to be in a talking mood tonight," Moses said. "I don't know if I'll get here again. But there's a gathering of white folks Saturday after next at the Smith plantation. Since the white folks will be occupied that day, I'll be at the quarters over there. If you need to find me, send word."

She began to stand up. Ben found himself rushing over to help her. She stared into his eyes and grabbed his hand. "Thank you, son. What's your name?"

"Ben, ma'am."

"Benjamin. That's a good name."

She walked toward the door and turned around, facing the silent people. "Be ready," she said. "Freedom is at hand."

Mistress Lowndes sat on the side of the canopy bed with the back of her hand on Mariah's forehead. "Get a cool rag for her face, Milly."

"Yes, ma'am." Milly descended the stairs and crossed the passageway to the kitchen.

Sophie stood at the counter. "What's she needing now?"

"Cool rag," said Milly. "Fever's back up."

Sophie shook her head. "Just used the last of the water for this broth. Sorry."

Milly grabbed the bucket and headed outside toward the well. The moon was setting, and the sun would be up soon. She hauled the water back to the kitchen.

Sophie was dumping hominy grits into a pan. "It's about time to get breakfast started, Milly. I'll see what I can do since you're busy."

Taking some rags and a pan of water, Milly headed back upstairs. Mistress put a cool rag on Mariah's forehead. Milly dampened another rag and dabbed at the girl's cheeks and neck.

Mistress Lowndes stood and looked out the window. "I believe Dr. Baker's finally coming, Milly. Go down and show him up to the room."

"Yes, ma'am." Milly waited on the veranda while Massa Lowndes and Dr. Baker rode up and dismounted.

Dr. Baker carried his black bag. "...course I'll have to take a look at her, but it sure sounds like malaria to me. Mosquitoes are especially bad this year."

Massa Lowndes nodded. "They've even pulled the troops back from the rivers and swamps."

Milly escorted the doctor to Mariah's room.

Mistress Lowndes met him at the door. "Dr. Baker, I'm so glad you're here."

Dr. Baker nodded. "Ma'am." He opened his bag as he walked over to the bed.

Mistress Lowndes dismissed Milly. By the time the sun was rising, Dr. Baker was gone and breakfast was ready.

Sophie stood at the kitchen table stirring a pan of grits. "Coffee's boiling, Milly."

"I'll get it," Milly said, taking the coffee off the fire. It felt like she was working in slow motion since she had never gotten to bed last night.

Sophie pulled the biscuits out of the oven. "You need to go fetch the milk, too."

By the time Milly was back from the dairy house, she heard a commotion in the Big House. She looked at Sophie. "Ain't that Ol' Man Pipkin's voice?"

"Don't know. Ain't none of my business."

Milly poured the milk into a glass pitcher. She put the milk and coffee on a tray and crossed the passageway from the kitchen to the Big House. The male voices were louder. She recognized Massa Lowndes saying, "Have you asked the others where they are?"

"They aren't talking. I can't get 'em to say anything," said the second voice. Was it Ol' Man Pipkin?

"They won't get far," said Massa Lowndes. "We'll deal with them after breakfast."

"I'll whip 'em good when I get 'em back." It was definitely Ol' Man Pipkin's voice. "So you want me to go on and...?"

"Go on and start everyone else working," said Massa Lowndes. "Just like a normal day. As I said, they won't get far."

Milly left the tray in the dining room and went

back to the kitchen. "Miss Sophie, somebody's done run off! I don't know who, but somebody's…"

"Hush your mouth, girl, and quit talking nonsense." Sophie dumped the grits into a serving bowl.

Milly edged up closer to Sophie. "I just heard Massa Lowndes and Ol' Man Pipkin talking about it."

"Ain't no concern of ours, Milly. Don't go starting no confusion. You gonna get in trouble some day with all this talk of yours." Sophie handed the breadbasket and butter to Milly, and they both carried food into the dining room.

Mistress Lowndes was already standing at the table talking to her husband when Milly and Sophie entered the room.

"Which ones escaped?" Mistress said.

"Big Joe and Sam."

Mistress raised her eyebrows. "Sam?"

"I couldn't believe it either. Sam's my most loyal…"

"What happened to Sam?" Susan interrupted, entering the room.

Massa and Mistress Lowndes looked at each other for a few seconds. Mistress finally answered, "Sam ran away. Big Joe's missing also."

"Let's sit down and have breakfast," Massa Lowndes said. "I've got a full day ahead of me."

They sat and Massa said the prayer. Milly started serving the coffee and milk, and Sophie left for the kitchen.

Mistress Lowndes spread butter on her biscuit. "I can't understand why Sam would run away."

Susan spooned grits onto her plate. "I know, Mother. He was the coachman, for heaven's sake. We treated him real well."

Massa Lowndes put down his cup and made a tent with his fingers. "I know one thing. When we bring him back, Sam won't be coachman anymore."

⭐

Chapter 10

SWING AND DIG

Ben's back was burning, and the hot sun wasn't even overhead yet. He swung the hoe, bringing it down between rows, digging up weeds, and loosening the dirt. Swing and dig, swing and dig. Everybody swung in the same rhythm.

Big Joe's scarred back was not in front of him today. Ben wondered where he was and how far he had gone. He must have left on Saturday night, Ben figured. *You have to leave when you ain't gonna be missed for the longest amount of time.* Massa Lowndes had called in help from the neighbors. Men and dogs had been arriving on the plantation all morning. Ben heard the hounds baying in the distance.

Ol' Man Pipkin's voice carried over the fields. "Get a move on! I want twice as much work out of you today, boy." Swing and dig, swing and dig.

Last night's prayer meeting had been uneventful, nothing at all like the one last week when Moses had shown up. But Ben had noticed Big Joe and Sam weren't there. There had been whispering among folks, people talking in hushed voices about the two men, but nothing was said outright.

Then there was the alarm in Ol' Man Pipkin's voice this morning when everyone reported for work. "Where's Big Joe?" he had yelled. "Where's Sam?"

Ol' Man Pipkin had gone down the line asking each person. Ben was glad when he could truthfully say, "I don't know, suh." Big Mama was trembling. Ben was surprised Big Joe and Sam had disappeared together since they'd never seen eye to eye. Maybe they both wanted freedom so much they didn't care about their differences.

Sweat was running into Ben's eye, and he tried to wipe it when his arm came down on the next swing. He missed. Swing and dig, swing and dig. He heard Ol' Man Pipkin's footsteps behind him. The sun burned. His eye stung with sweat. Swing and dig, swing and dig.

"Twice as much work out o' you today, I said." Ben could picture Ol' Man Pipkin's leathery face and his just-smelled-a-skunk look. "If some o' you gonna go running off, then the rest are gonna work harder. Twice as much work, I said."

Ben was so thirsty his tongue was sticking to the roof of his mouth. Pipkin was holding the water back too. Ben peeked under his arm as he swung the hoe and saw Thomas standing at the edge of the field with the water bucket. Another several minutes went by.

"Water boys!"

Ben stood up and stretched. Thomas came up the row with the water bucket. "Hey, Ben."

Ben took the tin cup and took two long gulps of cool water. He dipped the cup in the bucket for another drink but heard footsteps behind him.

"Who's this here?"

Ben turned to see Ol' Man Pipkin staring at Thomas. "You, boy. What's your name?"

"Thomas, suh."

"Thomas, you know what?"

"What, suh?" Thomas's voice was shaky.

"We got plenty of water boys. Plenty of 'em." Pipkin smiled, but the smile didn't reach his eyes. "You know what else, boy?"

"What, suh?" Thomas's eyes were filling with

tears.

"I believe you're now old enough to pick up a hoe. In fact, we got a couple of spare hoes now that ain't being used. Come with me, boy." Water sloshed out of the bucket as Ol' Man Pipkin grabbed Thomas by the arm and jerked him away. "Get back to work, all of you!" Pipkin yelled over his shoulder.

Swing and dig, swing and dig. Ben gripped the hoe with his fists. For a moment, he wondered what it would feel like to have Ol' Man Pipkin's neck in his hands instead of the hoe. Swing and dig, swing and dig. The hoe savagely tore into the soil. This is what Big Mama was talking about. When Solomon ran off, things got harder for everybody. Big Joe and Sam ran away, and things are getting harder for everybody else left behind.

Swing and dig, swing and dig. After a few more minutes, footsteps came up behind Ben, but he didn't break his rhythm.

"You get right here, boy." Ol' Man Pipkin shoved Thomas in front of Ben. "Watch the one in front of you. Swing that hoe when he swings." Thomas awkwardly swung the hoe. Ol' Man Pipkin stood in front of Ben. Pipkin manipulated his whip, folded it, then let it dangle at his side. "Now dig them weeds out. Use some muscle, boy! Get that weed up."

Swing and dig, swing and dig. Ben kept his eyes on the back of Ol' Man Pipkin's neck and clenched the hoe until his fingers were numb.

"I said dig up that weed, boy!" Pipkin hollered, as he unfurled the whip.

Thomas struggled with the hoe, but couldn't get the weed loose from the soil. The hoe was longer than he was tall.

Swing and dig, swing and dig. Ben couldn't stand it any longer. "Put your hands closer up on the hoe, like this," he told Thomas under his breath. Ben gripped the hoe half way up the handle.

Thomas tried it. He was finally able to dig up the weed.

Ben felt and heard it before he realized what happened. The harsh sting, the snapping sound, the slow dripping down his back, followed by Ol' Man Pipkin's sneering voice: "Boy, next time you talk when I don't ask you to, you'll get more than one lash." By the time Ben lifted his eyes to look at the overseer, Ol' Man Pipkin was looking at Thomas again.

"That's it. Keep on a-working, boy." Ol' Man Pipkin was chewing on a piece of straw and walking away.

Swing and dig, swing and dig. The footsteps were gone.

Ben glanced up. Thomas was struggling with the hoe. "Just try to stay with the rhythm, Thomas."

"It's heavy, Ben."

"I know. Stay with the rhythm. I'll try to help you with the weeds."

Swing and dig, swing and dig. Ben wondered where Big Joe was. He'd probably gone north. And Sam had probably headed south to Beaufort. He'd always wanted to join up and be a soldier. Sam might make it to Beaufort, since it wasn't that far away. Ben wasn't sure about Big Joe, though.

Swing and dig, swing and dig. Ben would love to run away just as Big Joe and Sam had done, but he now knew he wouldn't do it. As Big Mama said, it leaves a mess for the folk left behind. Ben had a weapon he could use against Massa Lowndes and Ol' Man Pipkin, though. If it helped the Union Army, it might set them all free. He had to be careful, though, or he'd get everybody in trouble and nobody would be saved. He didn't even know if Moses would be back to their plantation. He might have lost his chance when he didn't tell her during her visit last week. If he wanted to talk to her, he'd have to go to the

Smith plantation on Saturday. If he were caught off the Lowndes plantation, he would get whipped. He had to decide by Saturday if he was going to tell her or not.

Swing and dig, swing and dig. Maybe he should talk to Uncle Minus. Sometimes his old friend had a magic way of understanding the world, clearing up confusion and making decisions easier. After all, you don't get to be eighty-eight years old without learning a thing or two.

Swing and dig, swing and dig. Ben realized he didn't hear the hounds anymore.

That night, people spoke in hushed voices in the quarters about Big Joe and Sam.

"Big Joe ain't never gonna learn."

"Sam's headed south for sure."

"Ain't no way Big Joe would go south."

"They never got along anyway."

"They don't stand a chance with them hounds."

"Maybe if they stay in the rivers…"

And on and on. People kept listening to the night sounds, but nobody heard any hounds baying or men shouting. At dawn, a fine drizzle began falling. Ben preferred rainy days since the clouds kept the sun off his back. He listened all day for sounds of men or hounds, but he heard none and the land grew dark.

That night, people whispered again.

"This rain today might have helped 'em."

"Maybe Big Joe finally got away."

"By now, Sam should be in uniform."

"Maybe them hounds got lost," followed by snickering sounds muffled by hands.

The rain ended that night. Early the next morning, Ben and Thomas were working in the fields as the sun rose. They had only hoed a few rows when Ben thought he might be hearing—could it be?—yes, hounds were baying. Several minutes went by. The horn blew.

Thomas stopped hoeing and turned around. "Ben, what's that mean? It ain't time for the midday meal yet."

"Don't know, Thomas."

They walked back toward the Big House. Ol' Man Pipkin was standing on the veranda with his whip in one hand and Sam's arm in the other. Sam's hands were tied behind him, and he held his head down. Massa Lowndes stood off to the side of the veranda. Ol' Man Pipkin waited for everyone to gather before he spoke. "This boy tried to run away but didn't get very far." Pipkin chewed on a piece of straw. "Tried to run away to them Yankees. I'm telling you right now them Yankees'll sell you down to Cuba if they get hold of you." He let his whip unfurl at his side. "I want all y'all to know what happens to someone who tries to run away."

Ol' Man Pipkin shoved Sam forward. "Get over there by that tree, boy." Sam walked to the magnolia. The overseer reached in his pants pocket, drawing out a knife as he walked over to Sam. Pipkin slipped the knife under the rope on Sam's wrists and jerked it up, releasing him. "Put your hands on that tree, boy." Sam bent toward the trunk and grabbed it with his fingers.

Ol' Man Pipkin ambled back a few paces, flicking the whip up and down. He turned to face Sam. Pipkin's jaw jutted out, and he drew his arm back. Ben heard a loud, cracking sound and saw Sam flinch. He heard Big Mama gasp. Without a pause, Pipkin drew his arm back for a second lash. Crack! When he got to ten lashes, rivulets of blood began to trickle down Sam's back. When he got to fifteen lashes, Sam was having trouble standing and Ben heard Big Mama sobbing. Pipkin stopped at eighteen lashes because Sam fell.

Ol' Man Pipkin stood up straight again and faced the crowd. "That's what happens when you run away. And I'll have Big Joe at that tree before long." Pipkin doubled his whip and then let it dangle at his side. "Let me tell you something else. Anybody who even gets near the border of this plantation will be whipped. Now, get back to work, all of you!"

In the cabin that night, Sam lay stretched out on a pallet, and Big Mama was bent over him, cleaning the wounds. Ben brought in a fresh bucket of water.

Big Mama squeezed out the rag, and bloody water ran into the old bucket. "Ben, bring me my root medicines." Ben went to the kitchen shelf and pulled down her box of roots. Some were dried, and some had already been mixed with water or made into pastes. Ben had helped her dig some of the roots in the woods around the plantation.

Big Mama opened the wooden box and began applying a poultice to Sam's back. Thomas stood beside Ben and tugged on his shirt. "Sam gonna be all right, Ben?"

"He'll be okay, Thomas. Big Mama'll take good care of him."

"Are they gonna really catch Big Joe too?"

"Don't know."

Sam stirred. Big Mama paused and then continued applying the poultice to the next wound.

Thomas grabbed Ben's shirt again. "Are they going after Big Joe now?"

"Guess so. They've still got some hounds running after him."

"Didn't Big Joe and Sam run away together? How come they caught Sam and not Big Joe?"

"I don't know, Thomas. Maybe they went different..."

"Hush, you two," Big Mama said. "Sam's needing some quiet."

Sam was stirring again. He moaned and then

tried to speak. "Big Joe wanted to…"

Big Mama put her hand on his head. "Don't you go trying to talk, now. And don't worry about Big Joe none. Just lay there and rest."

Sam tried to raise his head again. "Big Joe went…north. He wouldn't go with me to…Beaufort." Sam lay his head down again and sighed.

It was laundry day. Milly stumbled over a tree root as she carried the heavy bucket from the well. Water sloshed out. In the kitchen shed, she added water to the washtub. The coals were hot, but it would be a while before the water was warm enough to use.

"You got that washtub ready yet?" Sophie yelled from the yard. She was hanging up clothes from the first batch.

"It's still heating, Miss Sophie," Milly said.

Sophie grunted. "I still gotta get that gumbo started for tonight's supper."

Milly helped Sophie with the hanging. "Don't know how these folks use so many clothes," Sophie muttered under her breath. "You'd think they must have five arms and six legs."

Milly snickered. "Ain't that the truth."

A horse whinnied in the distance. "Someone must be coming," Sophie said, dropping a shirt back in the basket. "Get some water on to boil in case we have to serve."

Milly rolled her eyes and headed toward the kitchen. "As if we ain't got enough to do."

When Milly returned from the well, Mistress Lowndes was leaning into the kitchen with her hand on the doorframe. "Sophie, you and Millie prepare some tea and bread for Colonel Heyward and serve it out on the veranda," she said, breathlessly. "As quickly as possible." She turned and disappeared.

Milly poured the water into the pot while Sophie sliced bread. "Glad I baked an extra loaf yesterday," Sophie said.

"Colonel Heyward," Milly said, preparing the teapot. "Wonder what he's doing here?"

"Now don't you go sticking your nose where it don't belong."

"I'm just wondering, Miss Sophie, that's all."

When the tea and bread were prepared, Milly placed everything on a tray and carried it to the veranda. Colonel Heyward stood next to Massa Lowndes at the porch rail, looking out over the fields. "This leg still gives me problems from time to time, but other than that, I can't complain," said Massa Lowndes. He turned around when he heard Milly approaching and gestured toward the chairs. "Have a seat, Henry."

Colonel Heyward sat and pulled out two cigars. Milly offered the tray to the colonel. He waved the cigars in the air and chuckled. "Guess we'll save these for afterwards, huh?" He took a cup and saucer, and Milly filled it with tea.

Colonel Heyward put his cup on the table. "How's Mariah doing, Oliver?"

Massa Lowndes smiled and sat down. "Much better, thank you. The fever seems to be gone." He made a tent with his fingers. "What brings you here today?"

"I heard about your loss."

Massa Lowndes took a cup and saucer, and Milly poured tea. "We got one of them back yesterday."

"That's what I heard. I'm glad." Colonel Heyward took a plate with a slice of bread from the tray. "I've heard some information about someone who's in these parts helping slaves escape. Thought it might interest you."

Massa Lowndes narrowed his eyes. "What do they know about him?"

"About *her*. It's a *woman*, Oliver. A *colored* woman. She's been helping slaves escape from several of the plantations around here."

Milly eased into the back shadows of the veranda. She took a rag out of her apron pocket and began wiping the serving cart.

Massa Lowndes stared into the distance as he considered what he had heard. He finally took a plate with a slice of bread. "Can't anybody catch her, Henry? After all, it's just a woman."

"Apparently, she's not that easy to find." Colonel Heyward took a bite of bread. "You know, I remember hearing about someone just like her that was helping slaves escape up in Maryland a few years ago. Name was Harriet Tubman. She had a hefty price on her head, and they never did catch her. I just wonder if this isn't..."

"Does she take 'em north?"

"She's been helping 'em get down to Beaufort. They've been joining the Union Army." Colonel Heyward took a sip of tea. "That's what I'm here to tell you, Oliver. You know that slave you call Big Joe? I heard she took him down to Beaufort."

Milly dropped her rag, but the two men didn't notice. She quickly retrieved it from the floor, her hand trembling.

Massa Lowndes hadn't touched his bread. He pushed the plate away and leaned forward with his head in his hands. "So he's already down in Beaufort in the Union Army?"

"That's what I heard." Colonel Heyward took another sip of tea. "If it's any consolation, the two slaves that escaped from my place are probably down there too. From what I hear, that woman has helped so many slaves escape they call her 'Moses.'"

★

Chapter 11

HIGH JOHN AND COTTONMOUTH CODY

Ben stuck his head in the cabin doorway. "Big Mama, I'll be back in a little while."

Big Mama turned around, holding a spoon in her hand. "Where you going this late at night?"

"To see Uncle Minus."

Big Mama laid her spoon down. Lowering her voice, she said, "What's wrong, Ben?"

Ben shrugged. "Nothing. Just wanna talk to him."

"Don't be too long. I know Ol' Man Pipkin's been working you hard. You need your sleep. You hear?"

"Yes'm."

Ben shuffled down the pathway along the cabins. He grabbed his right shoulder and rubbed it. The extra workload made his shoulder throb in the evenings.

Uncle Minus's cabin looked identical to all the other cabins. "Uncle Minus?" Ben called from the outside.

A woman's voice answered. "Come on in."

Daphne, Uncle Minus's daughter, sat by the fire weaving a mat. Uncle Minus sat next to her. Several other people slept on mats against the walls.

Uncle Minus saw Ben and gestured to the floor. "Come sit beside me."

Ben sat, still rubbing his sore shoulder.

Uncle Minus smiled. "I been expecting you."

Ben looked up at Uncle Minus. "What do you

mean?"

"Something's been troubling you."

"A lot's been going on."

"I hear Ol' Man Pipkin's been cracking down hard on y'all. Making you work extra long hours and twice as hard."

"Yes." Ben yawned. "He even started Thomas hoeing the other day."

"That a fact?"

Ben nodded. "He's too little to hold a hoe up straight, much less dig with one. Thomas was trying his best, and Ol' Man Pipkin was standing over him with his whip. I tell you, Uncle Minus, I could've reached over and put my hands around Ol' Man Pipkin's neck." Ben stared into his lap.

"Now, Ben, don't go doing nothing crazy like that."

"He was standing there with his face all wrinkled up and that scar under his eye," Ben continued. "His nose was turned up like it always is. Will calls it his just-smelled-a-skunk look."

Uncle Minus chuckled.

"He's one ugly creature," Ben said, shaking his head. "I don't know how I kept myself from putting my hands around his neck."

"It woulda just brung trouble. But I'll tell you how High John dealt with an ugly massa if you wanna hear."

Daphne interrupted. "Daddy, don't you think Ben's a little young for that story? People could get in trouble talking about an ugly massa."

Uncle Minus stuck his lips out at Daphne. "I always say if a child's old enough to ask questions about something, they's old enough to get the answer." He turned to face Ben. "Now, you wanna hear this story or not?"

Leaning back on his elbows, Ben smiled. "Sure, Uncle Minus."

The old man put his hands on his knees. "One day Ol' Massa finally got tired of John tricking him out of doing work all the time. He found a man down in Georgia interested in buying John.

"Now Ol' Massa was honest with the man. He told him, 'John's a healthy, strong slave, and he can do the work of four field hands—that is, if you can get him to do it. But most the time, John'll be telling you funny stories and making you laugh, and then, before you know it, the sun's gone down and ain't no work got done that day.'

"The man from Georgia was so mean they called him Cottonmouth Cody. He had a wrinkled face and a big ol' scar that ran from one cheek across his nose all the way to the other cheek. 'I ain't *never* had no trouble getting *my* slaves to work,' he told Ol' Massa. 'I ain't *never* had *no* reason to laugh, and I ain't *about* to start now.'

"Ol' Massa said, 'Well, I'm warning you to be careful 'cause John has a slippery tongue. Before you know it, he'll trick you into doing something you don't want to do.'

"Cottonmouth Cody nodded. 'I'll take my chances.'

"So Cottonmouth Cody took John to his plantation in Georgia. 'Now John, I want you to get out there and pick four hundred pounds of cotton today.'

"'Massa, that's just fine,' said John. 'But if I can make you laugh, won't you give me the day off?'

"Cottonmouth looked up at John and said, 'If you make me laugh, I'll not only give you the day off—I'll give you your freedom.'

"Then John walked back and forth in front of Cottonmouth Cody, gawking at his face.

"'What are you doing, boy?' said Cottonmouth.

"'I declare, Massa, you sure is a good-looking man!' said John.

"Cottonmouth stared back at John. 'I'm sorry I

can't say the same thing about you.'

John laughed. "'Oh, yes, Massa, you could,' he said. 'You could if you told as big a lie as I just told!'

"Before he thought about it, Cottonmouth was laughing out loud."

Uncle Minus held up a crooked finger.

Ben and Daphne joined in for the last line: "And THAT'S how John got his freedom!"

Uncle Minus stretched his legs out in front of him, still chuckling. "Feels good to laugh, don't it?"

Ben nodded. "Especially when there're people like Ol' Man Pipkin around."

"Sometimes, white people got reasons for acting mean and ugly, Ben. I been knowing Ol' Man Pipkin a long time. His daddy had land in these parts, and he owned some slaves. He treated 'em bad—he'd be whipping 'em all the time. Even killed a few of 'em, whipping 'em so hard. One of his slaves got tired of it and fought back one time. Ended up killing him."

"A slave killed Ol' Man Pipkin's daddy?"

"That's right. Years ago, when Ol' Man Pipkin was just a youngster."

"What happened to the slave?"

Uncle Minus stared into the fire, which was now little more than a bed of embers. "Lynched him. No trial or nothing."

Daphne added some wood to the fire and stirred it.

"Ol' Man Pipkin's held a grudge ever since," said Uncle Minus.

Ben sat up on his knees, grabbed a loose stick, and poked it into the fire. "Uncle Minus, what do you think about that woman Moses? You think she's really working with the Union?"

"Wouldn't surprise me. Sounds like they got a whole bunch of black soldiers down in Beaufort."

"She keeps asking us questions." Ben hesitated. "But if anybody told her what she wants—they'd probably get in trouble with Massa Lowndes, right?"

Uncle Minus stared at the boy for several seconds, his cloudy, brown eyes boring into Ben's. The old man seemed to be trying to read his thoughts. "Well," Uncle Minus said, "if Massa Lowndes found out, he wouldn't be happy about it."

Daphne looked at Uncle Minus out of the corner of her eye as she continued weaving.

Uncle Minus sighed. "Ben, there was a time when our only hope of freedom was to run north. You wouldn't dare be blabbing secrets to strangers. But times has changed since this war started. There's a chance we might all be set free. So things is different now."

"So you're saying it might be okay to risk being caught by Massa Lowndes?"

"Maybe. Depends on what you got to tell her and how useful you think it might be."

"Daddy..." Daphne began.

Uncle Minus held up his hand toward Daphne, simultaneously shaking his head. Daphne didn't continue.

Several seconds went by. "Big Joe always said whites are all the same—don't matter if they're Union or Rebel," Ben said. "He said the Union Army was just using Moses."

"Big Joe's bitter," Uncle Minus said. "He's afraid to believe anything good might happen. You notice he don't never listen to the High John stories. He don't even laugh when I'm telling one at a meeting.

"Them High John stories help keep bitterness at bay. If you let 'em, bitterness and hatred'll get into your thoughts and take over your life before you know it. High John's like a medicine for that. Them stories'll give you a good belly laugh. You get to poke fun at the overseer or the massa, and he never even know you're doing it. Just remember, boy, if you quit laughing, you quit living. Them stories keep hope alive." The old man pointed his finger at Ben. "I want to teach you them stories so you can pass 'em on."

"I'll try and learn 'em, Uncle Minus." Ben stared into the fire. "You think we'll ever see Big Joe again?"

"Don't know, Ben. Has Sam talked yet?"

"A little. He said he and Big Joe had split up— he had gone south to Beaufort and Big Joe had gone north."

Uncle Minus smiled. "Maybe Big Joe'll finally get his freedom."

"You think so?"

"Might never know, Ben. We can only hope."

The next day stretched on and on. Sunset was long past, and the western light still lingered. Ben figured he'd been in the fields about sixteen hours. Ol' Man Pipkin seemed to enjoy squeezing the last little bit of daylight out of everybody.

Thomas was adjusting better than Ben thought he would. His arm muscles had already grown stronger since he'd been hoeing, and Ben didn't have to rescue him by digging up his weeds as often.

Tomorrow was Saturday, and Massa Lowndes had already told Ol' Man Pipkin to make it a shorter workday. The Lowndes family was going to the Smith Plantation gathering, the same one that Moses had mentioned at her last visit. To most folks, the shorter workday meant a Saturday night gathering, a juba with fiddles and banjos. To Ben, it meant more time to make it to the Smith plantation slave quarters to find Moses—if he went.

The horn finally blew. Good thing too. It was getting so dark that Ben could barely see the rows of rice. He and Thomas walked toward the quarters. Big Mama came out of the cabin when she heard people coming.

"Ben, I already done the chores in the barn. You and Thomas come in and eat."

Ben and Thomas collapsed on the floor of the cabin and leaned against the wall.

"My body hurts all over," said Thomas.

Big Mama put soup and cornbread in front of them. Thomas began eating right away. Big Mama glared at Ben. "Come on, Ben. Don't give up on me now. You gotta eat."

Ben leaned forward and tore off a piece of corn-bread.

Big Mama shook her head. "I told you not to stay out late talking," she said, wiping her hands on her apron.

Ben ate the cornbread and a spoonful of soup. The soup was thin—Big Mama never had enough makings for the mouths she had to feed.

After he finished the meal, Ben spread his pallet on the floor and sat down to rub his feet.

Creeakk!! The cabin door opened.

Big Mama rushed over. "Milly, what're you doing here?"

Milly glanced at Ben, her eyes sending an urgent message. "Just came to have a word with Ben, that's all."

"Ben's too tired," Big Mama said, putting her hand on Milly's shoulder. "They been working 'em real hard in the fields. It'll have to wait till tomor-row."

"Won't take but a couple of minutes, Big Mama. I promise."

By then, Ben had made it to the door. "I'll talk to Milly outside," he told Big Mama. "I won't be long. I'll be right back."

As Ben and Milly disappeared into the night, they heard Big Mama muttering under her breath.

"Something wrong?" said Ben, walking away

from the cabin to make sure Big Mama wasn't eaves-
dropping.

"I don't have much time. Got to get back up to
the Big House. They don't know I'm gone."

Ben didn't answer.

Milly twisted a rag in her hands. "Colonel Heyward came over to talk to Massa Lowndes yesterday," Milly said. "I served tea, so I got to hear 'em
talk."

"So what did he say?"

"They know." There was urgency in Milly's voice.

"They know what?"

Milly grabbed Ben's arm. "They know about
Moses."

Chapter 12

THROUGH THE WOODS

On Saturday, the horn blew when the sun was still high off the horizon. People were in good spirits, talking with one another about the upcoming juba:

"Is Reuben gonna play his fiddle?"

"I hope so, 'cause I'm ready to dance."

"You bringing some of your stew?"

"Course I am. Already got it over the fire."

Ben and Thomas headed back toward the quarters and did their chores in the barn. By then, the fiddle music had started.

Dashing off, Thomas hollered, "I'm going to the juba."

"Better let Big Mama know," Ben answered. But Thomas was already gone.

Ben went down the row of cabins and peered into one toward the end. "Sam?"

A woman's voice answered. "Ben, is that you?"

He walked in. After the sun's glare, the cabin was dark and gloomy. For a moment, all Ben could see was a tiny flame in the center; then his eyes began to adjust. Kizzy, Sam's sister, was applying a poultice to her brother's back.

Ben nodded at the woman. "Hi, Miss Kizzy. How's he doing?"

Kizzy lowered her eyes. "Come on over. He can tell you himself."

Ben circled around, faced Sam, and stooped

down. "Hello, Sam."

"Hey, Ben."

"Feeling better?"

"I thought I was till Ol' Man Pipkin came in here today. He's making me go in the fields on Monday whether I'm ready or not."

"Sorry, Sam."

"No matter."

"Sam...I wanted to ask you something about Big Joe."

"Go on."

"You said he run north?"

"That's right. I wanted to go south to Beaufort, and he didn't want to go with me."

"Milly just heard something at the Big House— she heard them say Moses helped Big Joe get to Beaufort."

"Phew..." Sam lay his head down on his arms and didn't say anything else. The banjo had joined the fiddle outside.

"Do you think she really helped him get to Beaufort?" Ben said.

Sam raised his head. "She probably did." Laying his head on its side, he continued talking. "She wanted to help me get to Beaufort, but I wouldn't listen. Told me to leave a week later than I left, but I was itching to get out of here. Said the woods were full of Rebs."

"But if Big Joe was going north, why do you think she..."

"That's probably the only reason he wasn't caught. They been looking for people to go south to Beaufort—not north. Moses probably found him in the woods and talked him into going."

"I never thought Moses would talk Big Joe into going south."

"When you're tired and cold and wet and hungry, there's a lot of things you can be talked into."

Ben put his hand on Sam's shoulder. "Thanks, Sam. Hope you feel better."

Ben went out in the late afternoon sunshine and headed toward his cabin. He felt a light touch on his shoulder. It was Will.

"Hey, Ben, you staying around this afternoon for the juba?" Will asked, walking along beside him.

"I don't think so."

"Fishing?"

Ben stopped walking. "No."

"So where you going?"

Ben stared at Will for several seconds before answering. "I'm going over to the Smith plantation to find Moses. Gonna tell her about the torpedoes."

Will's eyes widened. "That means you're going off the plantation," he whispered. "You remember what Ol' Man Pipkin said?"

Ben sighed. "I thought you wanted me to tell her about the torpedoes."

"I never said I wanted you to go off the plantation to tell her."

"Don't worry, Will. I won't say nothing that'll get *you* in trouble."

Will raised his voice. "I ain't worried about that! What kind of friend do you think I am?"

"Shhh." What was Will thinking, blurting out so loudly? Ben looked around. Nobody seemed to have noticed. He put both hands on Will's arms. "This is something I got to do, Will. You understand?"

Ben pushed through the underbrush. A leaf chafed across his arm. The tip of a branch pricked his leg. Catching a whiff of something earthy, he looked on the ground and saw that an animal—maybe a fox—had been by and left some dung.

Ben heard a noise—a rustling in the leaves behind him. He froze. The rustling continued. Slowly turning around, he saw it was only a squirrel. When Ben faced forward again, he noticed an ant crossing a branch, carrying a heavy load several times its size. His every sense seemed to be heightened.

Ben saw the mill below him on his left. *Good. Making some progress.* He stayed in the woods to avoid being seen. But he kept the river in sight—just to make sure he was going in the right direction. *Lord, just let her be there,* Ben thought. He ducked under a low branch and had to lower his line and pole for a moment. He had brought his fishing gear for an excuse—just in case he got caught.

It was a relief now that Ben had made the decision. There'd be no turning back. A part of him wished he could have stayed with the others. Reuben would be playing his fiddle for hours, and Uncle Minus would be buck dancing. Before dark, Uncle Minus would be telling Br'er Rabbit stories; after the children went to bed, he'd pull out the High John tales.

But another part of Ben didn't want to stay. He hungered to strike out on his own and challenge himself. If he succeeded, he would help not only his friends and family but also lots of other people he didn't even know.

A tiny branch struck him in the face. The border of the plantation had to be somewhere around here. Ben's stomach growled. He hadn't bothered to grab anything to eat before he left. He kept pushing. Glancing downhill, Ben finally saw Colonel Heyward's fence across the river. He must be on Massa Smith's plantation.

Now things could get difficult. He didn't know where he was going. He'd keep following the river until he found a path, one that might lead to the Big House and slave quarters. He'd have to be careful about following a path, though. If he stumbled into some white folks, he'd get into trouble. He'd have to make sure that didn't happen.

Massa Smith's plantation didn't look any different from Massa Lowndes'. Same ol' underbrush. Same trees. Same squirrels. He'd been off Massa Lowndes' place one other time—the time he and Will had been swimming across the river. Somehow, this felt more dangerous. Maybe it was Ol' Man Pipkin's threats. If he and Will had been caught the time before, Pipkin might have believed that they were just a couple of boys going swimming. But Ben knew that Ol' Man Pipkin wouldn't believe any stories now.

Something snagged his pants, and he bent down to loosen it. Just a briar. As Ben stood again, he noticed a path crossing in front of him, leading down to the river. He looked to the right, and the path disappeared uphill into the woods. He stood still for a minute, listening closely. Satisfied that nobody was around, he turned right and took the path uphill. *Lord, just let her be there*, he thought.

Ben trekked through the underbrush. It was getting thinner. In the distance, he saw a clearing. Then he saw a building. He slowed his pace and listened. He heard distant voices laughing—white people. *Show me the quarters*, he thought. *Just show me the quarters.*

The path ended in back of one of the smaller houses. White folks seemed to have a house for everything—one for making soap, another for sewing, another for making furniture. There was a big kettle in front of this house, so maybe it was the soap-making house—he wasn't sure. He couldn't see the Big House. He had to turn right or left to look for the slave quarters. He went left.

The voices got louder. Yes, they were definitely white people. Ben hid behind trees, searching for people, houses, anything that would give him a clue. He went through the woods and came out behind another small house that appeared to be the wash house—clothes were hanging outside. The Big House was visible just beyond it. A crowd of white people in fine, fancy clothes had gathered on the veranda and the front yard of the Big House.

Ben ducked behind a big magnolia. Maybe he had gone the wrong way at the end of the path. He retraced his steps through the woods and behind the soap-making house. He kept going. Before long, he came to a small orchard. Beyond that, there were some small vegetable gardens. Finally, he saw two long lines of small one-room cabins, facing each other. *Lord, just let her be here*, he thought again.

Ben knew he wasn't completely safe yet. He'd heard stories of how slaves had sometimes told on other slaves. He had to be careful. The cabins seemed to be deserted today, though. At home, everybody was singing, playing music, dancing, and eating. Here, it was quiet as a graveyard. He eased down the middle of the row of cabins. No voices. He kept walking. At the end of the row, he heard a low murmur. He followed the sounds. Voices came from the cabin on the left, but the door was closed.

Ben decided to stay outside and wait. Surely it wouldn't be long. He walked behind the cabin and sat on the ground. After a few minutes, the voices became louder as if they were arguing about something. Some were male voices and some were female. Then a man began speaking—maybe praying—and then there was silence. After another moment, Ben heard an eerie and familiar voice:

> *When Israel was in Egypt's land,*
> *Let my people go!*
> *Oppressed so hard they could not stand,*
> *Let my people go!*
> *Go down, Moses*
> *Way down in Egypt's land.*
> *Tell Ol' Pharaoh*
> *Let my people go!*

Ben heard a shuffling noise, and then the door opened. He hid behind the cabin.

"Pray hard," Moses was saying to someone. "We don't know what we're gonna run into."

Ben peeked around the corner. People were leaving the meeting, milling about, and visiting. He saw Moses heading into the woods by herself. Ben stood on his toes, preparing to slip away and follow her. Then a voice startled him.

"Ezra feeling better?" It was a woman's voice. And it came from the side of the cabin.

"He's about the same," another voice answered. Footsteps approached. Ben crouched behind the cabin until the voices faded. Then he glanced around the corner. Seeing no one, he rushed into the woods, heading for the spot where Moses had disappeared. He saw no sign of anybody. He walked a little farther. Then he stood still, catching his breath. He heard nobody. Should he risk calling her name?

"Moses!" It was half whispered, half spoken.

He looked right and left.

Then a voice came from behind him. "What're you doing on this plantation?"

⭐

Chapter 13

NOTHING TO LOSE

Ben turned around. It was Moses.

"Benjamin, isn't it?" she said.

"Yes'm," Ben answered, letting out a long breath. "I need to talk to you."

Ben told her everything—about the Rebel soldiers and the strange dark shapes he had found floating near the riverbank. After he finished, Moses stooped over with a stick in her hand, pointing toward the crude drawing in the sandy soil. "So there's one here...and here...and here...and here. Is that right?"

"Yes'm," said Ben.

"Them soldiers—they said there was ten of 'em?"

"Yes'm, I know they said they was supposed to have all ten of 'em in the river by the end of April."

"Well, you described the four you know pretty good. I think I can find 'em."

"I could maybe show 'em to you sometime," Ben offered.

Moses grunted and shook her head. "Ain't enough time. But you been a big help, Benjamin."

"I's wondering if I could ask you something, ma'am."

"Go on."

"Big Joe. Do you know where he is?"

Moses eyed Ben for a moment. "Down in Beaufort."

"Sam said he went north."

Moses didn't answer.

"Did you talk him outta going north?"

Moses smiled. "I come across him in the woods. He'd been sticking to the waterways mostly, trying to keep away from the hounds. But he was getting tired and hungry. I talked to him a long time. Told him some stories about people I've helped get away from slavery."

"You've helped people run away?"

"A few. I been doing it a while. Mostly taking people north. But now things has changed. Since the black man can fight, we have a chance of winning our freedom. That's why I been helping people get to Beaufort."

"Do they take somebody my age in the army?"

Moses smiled and put her hand on Ben's shoulder. "You been pretty useful where you are."

"But..."

"The sun's getting low, Benjamin. You best be getting back before they miss you."

Ben looked around. The trees must be blocking the western horizon. He wondered how Moses could even see the sun in the woods. She seemed to have an extra sense about those things.

Moses led him on a path, and they came out at the mill on Massa Lowndes' plantation.

"You know your way from here," she said. "Hurry up...and goodbye."

"Tell Big Joe hello for me."

"I will," she said. "Maybe you'll see him again before long."

Ben rushed through the woods. Colors were fading, and it was difficult to see. The music and dancing would be over, everyone would be back in their cabins, and Big Mama would be worried and upset. A briar snagged his pants leg, and he bent down to release it. Up ahead, he heard the barking of dogs. He stopped running. He didn't hear any voices. He started up again at a slower pace. A tiny branch slapped him in the face.

He came up to the magnolia where he usually met Will and turned toward the quarters. The hounds were much louder now, but he still didn't hear any voices. Maybe someone else had escaped. Since nobody was around, he shouldn't have any problem getting to the cabin without being seen. He walked uphill toward the barn.

A silhouette emerged from the corner of the barn and stood, facing him. Ben froze. It was an unmistakable figure—a thin man with a whip dangling from one hand.

"I don't know where you been, boy, but it wasn't on this plantation," said Ol' Man Pipkin, as he swaggered forward.

Ben couldn't talk. He still had his line and pole in his hand, and he vaguely remembered that his prepared excuse had something to do with fishing. He couldn't get his mouth to form the words.

"Come up here, boy." Pipkin grabbed Ben's arm and jerked him uphill. Ben stumbled, trying to follow him. On the other side of the barn, three hounds were tied. A crowd of slaves had gathered, and Ben saw Big Mama in the crowd. She raised her hands to her face when she saw him, and Ben lowered his eyes.

Ol' Man Pipkin shoved Ben away. "Take off your shirt and get over there, boy. You know where to go."

Ben removed his shirt and walked toward the old magnolia tree. He placed his hands on the furrowed, gray bark. He heard Ol' Man Pipkin snapping the whip a couple of times—he was getting warmed up.

It would have helped if he had known how many lashes he was going to get. But that was part of the plan, part of the torture.

Crack! He heard a gasp—his own.

Crack! He'd forgotten how much it stung. He

103

leaned his head on his arm, waiting for the next one.

Crack! Blood dripped down his back.

It kept going. He lost count. Beads of sweat popped out on his forehead.

Crack! His eyes filled up. *Lord, keep me from crying*, he thought.

He waited, but the rhythm was broken. Nothing happened.

"Get back over here, boy."

Ben lowered his hands. For a moment, he saw nothing, stooped over, almost fell. Someone had rushed over to catch him. A pair of arms helped him stand, and when he could see again, he stumbled toward the overseer.

Ol' Man Pipkin grabbed Ben's shoulder. "You're more trouble than you're worth, boy. You make sure you're back in the fields Monday morning, you hear?" Pipkin pushed Ben away.

A few minutes later, Ben was lying face down in his cabin, and Big Mama was washing his back.

"Will, could you get me some fresh water?" Big Mama said.

"Sure."

Thomas stooped down in front of Ben's face. "Ben, were you trying to find Mama?"

Ben's tongue kept sticking to the roof of his mouth when he tried to answer. "No, Thomas, I didn't..."

"Thomas, quit worrying him right now. Can't you see he's having enough problems?"

Thomas sulked away.

Will returned with the water.

"Get that gourd over there, Will, and dip some water for him."

The coolness and wetness of the water felt good on Ben's lips. He hadn't had anything to eat or drink all day. Big Mama continued washing Ben's wounds.

Ben tried talking again. "Will, how many lashes…?"

"How many?" Will said. "Ten. He gave you ten."

Ben spent Sunday lying face down on his pallet, with Big Mama bringing him water and soup throughout the day. He hated missing the prayer meeting that night.

Morning came too soon, and his back was so sore, he couldn't wear a shirt. Big Mama put medicine on him before he staggered out to the fields with his hoe. He had a longer walk than usual because he was working in the rice fields overlooking the Combahee River that day.

"I'll tell you what," Thomas told Ben. "You get in front of me, and I'll dig any weeds you can't get."

Ben smiled and reached over to pat Thomas on the head. The first blush was in the eastern sky. It would be another half hour before they would be able to see colors.

The horn blew and the hoeing began. Swing and dig, swing and dig. As Ben stretched his arms and dug into the earth, he could feel the wounds on his back reopening. A few droplets tickled his skin. Before long, Ol' Man Pipkin came strolling behind Ben.

"Just thought I'd check and make sure you were out here this morning, boy."

Swing and dig, swing and dig.

Ol' Man Pipkin hadn't moved. "You know, boy, I meant what I said about you being more trouble than you're worth."

Swing and dig, swing and dig. *What's that supposed to mean?* Ben wondered.

The minutes seemed like hours, and the hours seemed like days. Ben might as well have been trying to swing a hoe underwater. When the horn blew at nightfall, he felt like collapsing before he walked back to the cabin.

Thomas took his hand. "Come on. I'll help you."

Ben stumbled back. Maybe some water, soup, and cornbread would help.

Big Mama met them at the cabin door with a gourd of water. "Here's some water, Ben."

"Thanks," said Ben taking a drink. Then he tried to go in the cabin, but Big Mama blocked his way. She had her apron pulled up in her hands, and she was wringing it like a rag. Her forehead was wrinkled.

"Ben, Massa Lowndes wanna see you right away up at the Big House," said Big Mama, her voice trembling.

He turned and stared at the Big House off in the distance. Ol' Man Pipkin was standing on the veranda. Ben finished the water and handed the gourd back to Big Mama.

He took his time walking to the Big House and up the front stairs. Ol' Man Pipkin stood at the top with a smirk on his face but said nothing. He stood aside as Ben walked through the door.

Inside, Milly was waiting. "Stay here, and I'll get Massa Lowndes," she said before disappearing.

In another moment, she was back with Massa Lowndes. Ben noticed her eyes were full of tears before she turned to leave.

Massa Lowndes leaned on his cane. "Ben, you disappeared from the plantation on Saturday evening."

So that's what this was about. "I went fishing, suh."

"But you weren't supposed to go off the plantation. Mr. Pipkin made it a strict rule you weren't to go near the border of the plantation."

Ben stared at his feet. "Guess I got lost, suh."

"Boy, this makes two times you've been in trouble. You've run off twice. I don't like that."

"I'm sorry, suh. I won't do it again."

"Well, I'm going to make sure of that. That's why I called you up here. I've got a man in Georgia who's interested in buying you."

Ben felt his throat tighten. "Buying me, suh?"

"He's coming to look at you later this week. I've told him about you running off twice, but he thinks he can handle that. He says he never has trouble with any of his slaves."

Ben couldn't talk.

"He'll be looking at you so we can settle on a price. Now you go on back, and do a good job this week out in the fields."

Ben turned and walked out the door. Maybe he was dreaming and would wake up soon. He stumbled down the stairs, back to the quarters, and into the cabin. Thomas had already fallen asleep.

Big Mama turned around immediately, asking him questions with her facial expressions. When he didn't speak, she brought some water and soup and sat beside him. After a few bites, she put her hand on his arm.

Ben looked into her eyes. "He's selling me."

"No!" Big Mama buried her face in her apron. Her shoulders began shaking as she wept.

He finished his meal and lay on his pallet. Big Mama put medicine on his back. The hard part— telling her—was over. Now he had to live with it, that was all.

He should have run. If he had only known, he could have run away on Saturday with Moses. Now his chance was gone. Sure, he didn't want to leave his family behind. Now he was being torn from his family, so that didn't matter anyway. He had worked so hard to help his family and friends. He gathered all the information about the torpedoes. He had risked so much, thinking he was helping the Union Army. Now, when it was all said and done, none of it mattered. He was being sold to somebody way off in Georgia. He'd never see Mama or Milly or Thomas. He'd never see Big Mama or Uncle Minus or Sam. He'd never see anybody he knew again.

Maybe he could still escape, Ben thought. The man is coming later this week. Maybe he could run off before then. He had nothing to lose at this point. Sam had said that Big Joe got so far because they expected people to run south to Beaufort. Ben imagined the drinking gourd again, and in the darkness, he saw the front two stars pointing their way to freedom.

He would stay in the waterways as much as possible to throw off the hounds. Ben saw himself running through the water, then along the riverbank. Up ahead, he saw a boat on the edge of the river. Someone was leaning over the side, stretching out a hand, reaching for him. A soldier. Something seemed familiar about him.

As Ben approached the boat, he reached out, trying to run faster. Now he recognized the soldier: It was Big Joe, dressed in Union blue.

The hounds howled in the distance. Ben was running, running through the muck, through quicksand, and each step became more cumbersome. The hounds were baying close behind him now, about to overtake him. He was almost touching Big Joe's hand...

Ben awoke with his heart pounding. Another nightmare.

★

Chapter 14

COMMOTION ON THE COMBAHEE

The next morning, Big Mama put medicine on Ben's back and gave him some food before he shuffled out the door with Thomas. They walked to the fields overlooking the Combahee.

The horn blew and the hoeing began anew. Swing and dig, swing and dig. At first, it was so dark he could barely see the weeds in the rows of rice. As he worked, pinks, purples, and blues spread into the black eastern sky.

Ben wondered where Moses was and if he could somehow find her. He had to think of a way to escape before the man came from Georgia. Maybe if he left as soon as he got off work today—it might be his only chance. He glanced up at the cloudless sky. If it remained clear, he would be able to see the stars tonight.

Swing and dig, swing and dig. In the distance, he heard Ol' Man Pipkin hollering about something. The sun peeked up over the horizon.

Then Ben heard footsteps. Not the slow, swaggering footsteps of Ol' Man Pipkin but a loud thudding sound. At the same time, he heard heavy panting as the footsteps came closer. Ben paused in mid-swing and saw Sam approaching, gasping for breath.

Sam stopped in front of Ben. "Two gunboats…" Sam leaned over and put his hands on his knees. He was breathing too hard to finish.

Ben looked around for Ol' Man Pipkin and didn't

see him. "What's the matter, Sam?"

"I saw two gunboats coming up the river."

"Union? Rebel? Who is it?" But Sam had already run off.

"What's that mean, Ben?" Thomas said.

Ben stood with his hoe resting on his shoulder. "I ain't sure."

Moments later, a steamboat whistle blew. The rhythm in the field was broken, and heads rose up everywhere. One gunboat, with a flag flying high, came slowly churning into view. The upper deck was crowded with people.

Some of the field workers ran back toward the quarters. Thomas grabbed Ben's hand. "Why're people running, Ben?"

"They getting scared, I guess. Maybe they's afraid it's the Rebels."

"Is it?"

"Don't know, Thomas."

Seeing no trace of Ol' Man Pipkin, Ben thought about people he needed to find. Big Mama and Uncle Minus would be back at the quarters and wouldn't even know about the gunboats. And Milly—she was in the Big House.

The boat approached the riverbank and tied off at the mouth of Jack's Creek. Soldiers filed out and came ashore, marching up the causeway. At first, Ben was too busy noticing that the soldiers were black to see the color of their coats.

Ben smiled. "Wouldja look at that?"

Thomas pulled on Ben's hand. "Are they Union or Rebel?"

"Well, they got blue coats. Look at those bright red pants! I'd say they's Union soldiers from Beaufort."

As the soldiers came ashore, another boat kept advancing up the middle of the river.

"Everybody run to the woods and hide!" It was

Ol' Man Pipkin's voice. He was running back and forth across the field. "Do you hear me? Run to the woods and hide!" He came closer, and Ben crouched down. "If the Yankees catch you, they'll sell you to Cuba. Run now!" Pipkin said.

Pipkin's words inspired people to move. However, instead of following his orders, most ran toward the gunboat, hoping to be rescued.

"Come on, Thomas, we gotta tell Big Mama." Ben pulled Thomas back toward the quarters. They ran against the tide of people flocking toward the river. *I get the feeling I'm going the wrong way*, Ben thought. He looked frantically around him, wondering if Big Mama was already heading toward the boat.

"Come on," he heard one man say, running toward the river. "Mr. Lincoln's gunboats done come to set us free!"

At the quarters, women were packing their belongings and hurrying away with baskets on their heads. A woman scurried by carrying a live chicken. Ben entered his cabin and found it empty. *Why can't this be easier? I've got to get on that boat.* He went to the corner where he slept, reached under his pillow, and pulled out the handkerchief his mother had sent. He stuffed it in his pocket.

With Thomas stumbling behind him, Ben ran down to Uncle Minus's cabin.

He pushed the door open. "Uncle Minus?" It was dark, and it took Ben's eyes a moment to adjust.

Big Mama was helping Uncle Minus stand. "Ben, help me get Uncle Minus down to the boat. Daphne's taken the children."

Ben got on one side and Big Mama on the other. He hesitated. "Can I see if Will's in his cabin?"

"Will came to get his mama," she said. "Come on, Ben. Time's a-wasting. We gotta go before the boat leaves us."

As they helped Uncle Minus across the fields,

they noticed great clouds of black smoke billowing in the air.

Reaching the rice fields in front of the boat, Uncle Minus asked them to stop. He stared at the soldiers. "Look at them black soldiers. Look at 'em! They so presumptuous, coming right ashore and holding their heads up high!" He laughed and started walking toward the river again. On the bank, they waded through the shallow water to the boat.

"I can help him up," said a familiar voice. A hand reached down. Ben looked up into the face of Moses. Next, she helped Big Mama and Thomas climb into the boat. Then Moses held out her hand for Ben.

He hesitated. "My sister's up at the Big House. I gotta get her."

Moses was silent for a moment. "I understand," she said.

Ben turned around and faced the plantation. Smoke seemed to be rising from everywhere. Soldiers were returning to the boat, and a throng of people rushed to the river, clamoring to get on board.

He ran uphill toward the Big House. *Crack. Crack.* Rifle shots rang out. Ben crouched, looked ahead, and saw a couple of Rebel soldiers. He glanced at the Big House. One of the soldiers was between him and the House.

Boom! A cannon went off on the gunboat behind him. He looked back—the last of the Union soldiers were getting on board. He was almost out of time.

He'd have to go the long way—through the woods—to the Big House. He turned to his left and crawled on the ground, trying to reach the trees. He glanced up at the House again. It looked like somebody might be—yes, somebody was running from the House. Milly. It was Milly!

"Stop right there!" Ol' Man Pipkin shouted, perching on a rock with a pistol in his hand. "You come back here!"

But Milly kept running. By now, she was in the rice field not too far from Ben. Ol' Man Pipkin took aim and fired. Milly fell to the ground.

Without thinking, Ben ran toward her. He had almost reached her when he heard another gunshot. Looking uphill, he saw Ol' Man Pipkin with his pistol pointed toward a group of slaves, forcing them back toward the cabins.

Ben reached Milly. "Ben," she said, turning around, "my arm..." The bloody sleeve was ripped open.

"Don't look too bad," he said, removing his shirt. "Looks like it's grazed."

He wrapped his shirt around her arm, tying it in place.

"Come on," Ben said.

They heard more gunshots. Glancing uphill, they two saw the soldiers were aiming at the gunboat. Ben helped Milly stand, and they ran to the river-bank.

Moses helped them climb into the boat. "This your sister?"

Ben nodded. "Milly."

"You stay here with me," Moses told Milly, glancing at her arm. "I'll take a look at that later."

Boom! The cannon on the boat went off again.

Uncle Minus stood on the boat watching the commotion. "I's eighty-eight year old, but I's never too old to leave the land of bondage." Big Mama stood beside him, nodding.

Ben grabbed Thomas's hand and scanned the boat. "Thomas—you see Will?"

Thomas looked up at him. "All I see's a bunch of legs."

Ben squeezed past a woman pointing in the distance. "Look, they set fire to the mill," she shouted.

"And Massa's barn—ten thousand bushels of rice—all in a blaze!" another voice said.

Ben felt a hand on his shoulder. "Hey, Ben." It was Will.

Ben felt his whole body relaxing. "I was worried about you, Will."

The boys watched the spectacle. People thronged the riverbank, hoping to be rescued. One woman, with twin girls hanging around her neck, hurried toward the boat, carrying a squawking chicken in a bag.

"Look at that!" Will said, pointing to another woman. She had three children clinging to her long dress and another child on her shoulders. She carried a bag with a pig in one hand. Her other hand balanced a pail of rice on her head. While the woman struggled to make it to the boat, the child on her shoulders was scooping rice into his mouth.

"I can't see," Thomas said, jumping up and down. Ben lifted Thomas onto his shoulders. They were shoved back and forth as people filed past. The Rebels fired their guns, and the boat's howitzer cannon occasionally thundered a reply. Moses was still helping people climb onto the boat. The steam whistle blew, and a soldier shouted, "Get ready! We're pulling away."

"Ben, look at Miss Kizzy!" Thomas yelled. Kizzy was stumbling toward the boat with a child and two piglets in tow. "Those are the piglets we been feeding!"

Moses jumped down off the boat to help her.

"Double-quick," one of the soldiers commanded.

Moses took the piglets, tucking one under each arm. As she attempted to climb back on the boat, Moses stepped on the hem of her long dress, tearing a gaping hole. "Lord o' mighty! I gotta quit wearing this long thing and get me one of them bloomer dresses," she said, glancing down at the shredded material. Kizzy then climbed on board with her child.

The boat pulled away from shore and began to steam downriver, packed with a cacophony of chattering people, squawking chickens, and squealing pigs. The steam whistle sounded again.

A voice thundered from the upper deck. "Moses, you'll have to give them a song!" A tall, white man with a wrinkled face and bushy side-whiskers stood in a blue uniform. His gaze was fixed on Moses, who sang:

> *Of all the whole creation*
> *In the East or in the West*
> *The glorious Yankee nation*
> *Is the greatest and the best*
> *Come along, come along*
> *Don't be alarmed*
> *Uncle Sam is rich enough*
> *To give you all a farm*

"Who's that woman?" someone asked one of the soldiers.

"Harriet Tubman," he said. "But most folks just calls her Moses."

"Let's go see the piglets!" Thomas said, sliding down from Ben's shoulders and pulling him by the hand. The young animals were chasing each other, drawing a crowd of laughing onlookers.

"I'm glad you brought the piglets," Ben told Kizzy.

"They's yours," she said. "Since you was raising 'em, I didn't see no reason to leave 'em for Massa Lowndes!"

One of the soldiers stooped down to pet one of the piglets. "They got names yet?"

"No," said Ben.

The soldier smiled. "Then let's call the white one Beauregard and the black one Jeff Davis!" The other soldiers laughed.

"Well, look who's here," Ben heard a familiar voice behind him. He turned and saw Big Joe, dressed in a blue coat, kepi, and red pants.

Ben smiled. "Moses said you went to Beaufort."

Big Joe nodded. "I changed my mind about going north."

Leaning over the side rail of the boat, they watched the big flames and huge columns of smoke rising. Big Joe's forehead creased and his tone changed. "Looks like you got in trouble with Ol' Man Pipkin." He gestured toward Ben's bare back.

"I ran off to Massa Smith's to find Moses," said Ben. "I knew where four of the torpedoes were."

Big Joe nodded. "She told me about that. We'd never made it upriver if we hadn't knowed where them things was. These boats woulda been blown to pieces."

"I'm glad y'all came when you did," said Ben. "Massa Lowndes was gonna sell me."

Will walked up on the other side of Big Joe and leaned over the rail.

"Glad I got away," said Big Joe. "Just wish I coulda seen Ol' Man Pipkin's face when them boats came up river."

"He had that just-smelled-a-skunk look on his face—like always," said Will.

"He was running back and forth yelling, 'Run to the woods and hide! If the Yankees catch you, they'll sell you to Cuba!'" Ben said.

Big Joe laughed out loud. And at that moment, Ben realized he had never heard him laugh before.

Big Joe smiled at Will. "Just-smelled-a-skunk look, huh? Now that you mention it, he *does* always look like he's come across something that stinks."

"That reminds me," said Ben. "Uncle Minus told me a story about High John and the ugly massa. You know that one, Big Joe?"

Big Joe shook his head. "Don't know that one. Can you tell it?"

"I think so," he said. As the gunboat continued

down the Combahee, Ben told the story to Big Joe and Will.

★

Chapter 15

THE HARRIET WEED

Ben stood on deck, watching slaves on the riverbank run toward the boat, some with huge bundles on their heads. People hollered as the boat passed by. Although Ben couldn't understand their words, he understood their meaning and wondered if his mother was among them.

Moses cleaned and bandaged Milly's wounded arm while Sam questioned Big Joe about the regiment. "So you're only in Beaufort for a couple of days?" Sam asked.

"Think so," Big Joe said, "but Colonel Montgomery's not saying for sure."

"You think that's enough time for me to join?" asked Sam.

Big Joe smiled. "We always got time for new people."

The boat was crowded; even so, it stopped to take on a few more people. Perhaps Moses or Colonel Montgomery, the white officer on the upper deck, took pity on them. Ben pushed his way forward to see these people. He anxiously watched as Moses helped them board, but his mother was not among them. He figured they must have passed the Kirkland plantation by now.

As the boat approached a bluff on the riverbank, Ben noticed a man waving his hat in the air.

"Who's that, Big Joe?"

"That's Capt'n Carver. We left him with his

company here at Tar Bluff on the way up." The boat stopped to let the soldiers board before churning on down the river.

Boom! Boom! The cannons bid a final farewell as they continued downstream toward Beaufort. Dark thunderclouds threatened in the west and blew in quickly. Heavy rain fell that night. Ben found Big Mama, Milly, and Thomas and sat with them on deck. Time passed, and he found himself sopping wet, leaning against Big Mama, and not entirely sure if he was awake or asleep.

The next thing Ben knew, Milly was shaking him awake. "Ben, look!" Someone stepped on his foot as people rushed past.

Ben stood and looked over the rail. The rain had stopped, and the sun was rising. They were pulling into a town, where a cheering crowd had gathered on the shore.

Big Joe walked up behind them and put his hand on Ben's shoulder. "Well, Ben, we made it to Beaufort."

"Wasn't there another gunboat, Big Joe?"

"It's the *Harriet Weed*," he said. "We're on the *John Adams*."

"Will there be people on that boat too?"

"There surely will," Big Joe said, nodding. "They stopped at other plantations."

"Wonder what's gonna happen to us," Milly said, her voice betraying some anxiety.

"They'll take you to a resettlement camp on one of the islands," Big Joe said. "Moses showed me one of them camps. People live in cabins and work for wages—no more slaving for the massa. Some of 'em even got schools."

Ben raised his eyebrows. "You mean I could learn to read and write?"

"That's right," said Big Joe. He glanced behind him and saw the soldiers gathering on the other side of the boat. "I might not be seeing you for a while 'cause we're heading out in a couple of days." He stuck his hand out.

Ben shook it. He felt his eyes begin to sting and turned his face downwards. Big Joe wrapped his big arms around Ben, hugged him, and then held him at arms' length. He tilted Ben's face up.

"Look at me, Ben."

Ben locked eyes with Big Joe, but he couldn't talk.

"Thanks, Ben. Thanks for everything." Big Joe walked off, joining the soldiers.

The steam whistle blew, and the boat pulled into the dock. People started going ashore. Ben jumped down and helped Big Mama, Milly, and Thomas get off the boat.

"This way, folks. Everybody, come this way," a man shouted, herding them into a crowd of bodies.

Ben grabbed Big Mama's hand. "I wanna find the *Harriet Weed*."

Big Mama's eyebrows knitted together. "Find the what?"

"The *Harriet Weed*. The other boat," said Ben, dropping her hand and taking off in the opposite direction.

"How we gonna…? Ben…stop!"

Ben ignored Big Mama, winding his way against the tide of people. He passed the *John Adams* and kept going. The harbor shoreline turned, and he noticed another boat docking. He couldn't read the name on the side, but it was overflowing with black people, including black soldiers.

Ben heard Big Mama come up behind him, breathing heavily. "I thought I'd lost you," she said, holding Milly and Thomas by the hand.

Ben pointed. "I think this is it." He scanned the people on the boat, as it crept up to the dock and tied off. After a long delay, people began filing out.

Big Mama put her arm around Ben, and they stood together, watching.

"I can't see," Thomas said.

Ben sighed, picking Thomas up.

"There, I think," Milly said softly, pointing. "In the back."

Ben followed her gaze. Was it really...? Yes, it had to be her. It was Mama.

By the time his mother was ready to climb ashore, Ben had put Thomas down and moved beside the gangplank to help her. He reached toward her.

Mama raised her hands to her face. "Ben?"

"Come on, Mama!" said Ben. "What are you waiting for?"

She laughed, grabbed his hand, and climbed off the boat, pulling Ben into a strong embrace. Then she loosened her grip but kept one hand on Ben's arm. "Oh no, what happened, baby?" she said, gazing at Milly's arm.

Milly shrugged. "Ain't nothing," she said. "Just a run-in with Ol' Man Pipkin."

"Mama, don't forget me!" Thomas said.

Mama made a sound—something between laughing and crying—as she opened her arms, pulling Thomas and Milly into a hug. Ben was caught in an uncomfortable squeeze in the middle, but he didn't mind. When Mama finally let go, Ben noticed her face was streaked with tears. He reached in his pocket, pulling out the handkerchief she had sent. The gesture brought on a new flood of tears, as she gave Ben another hug.

Mama finally let go, dabbing at her eyes with the handkerchief. Then she took Big Mama's hands and squeezed them. "Thanks for taking care of my children, Hannah."

Big Mama wiped away a tear. "Weren't no trouble, Martha."

Thomas and Milly held Mama's hands as she

walked toward the church, with Ben and Big Mama following. Ben leaned over to Big Mama. "So I weren't no trouble, huh?"

Epilogue

NOTES FROM THE AUTHOR

During the Civil War in 1862, the Union (Yankee) soldiers took Port Royal Island, just off the coast of South Carolina. Southern landowners fled, abandoning their plantations and slaves. Union troops set up camps to care for the slaves, and they urged teachers and nurses to come to the area. Many northerners responded, including Harriet Tubman.

Tubman had been born a slave on the eastern shore of Maryland. She had almost died as a teenager when an overseer threw a stone or iron weight that struck her on the head. For the rest of her life, she suffered from seizures—frequent episodes in which she would fall asleep. These spells would happen without warning, and until she awoke on her own, nobody could arouse her.

Harriet Tubman was already famous in the north for her work as a conductor on the Underground Railroad. Because she had freed as many as 300 slaves from bondage, some people called her "Moses."

Many of the southern slaves on Port Royal Island, however, had never heard of her. These slaves spoke the "Gullah" language, a blend of English and various African languages. Harriet had difficulty communicating with them at first.

After Tubman arrived on Port Royal Island, she worked as a nurse, treating malaria and many other diseases. The malarial parasite is transmitted

123

by mosquitoes, and swamps are an ideal breeding ground. Patients have episodes of fever, chills and headache. African Americans sometimes carry a genetic trait that helps protect them from malaria. As a result, slaves along the Combahee plantations did not succumb to the disease as often as white people.

Tubman later worked as a spy by finding out where the Rebels had planted torpedoes in the Combahee River. She was then asked to plan and carry out an expedition up the Combahee River to destroy railroads, bridges and other property.

In 1863, African Americans were finally allowed to fight in the Union Army. Colonel James Montgomery organized the Second South Carolina Colored Volunteers, and these soldiers accompanied Harriet Tubman up the Combahee River.

Three gunboats—the *John Adams*, the *Harriet Weed*, and the *Sentinel*—left Beaufort, South Carolina, on the evening of June 1, 1863. Montgomery and Tubman were on the *John Adams*. The *Sentinel* got stuck on a sandbar a few miles upriver, but the *John Adams* and the *Harriet Weed* continued about 25 miles up the Combahee.

Early on the morning of June 2, the *Harriet Weed* anchored, while the *John Adams* continued upriver to Combahee Ferry where the soldiers destroyed a bridge. They also flooded rice fields and burned rice, corn, cotton, barns, mansions, storehouses and mills. Over 700 slaves flocked to the gunboats and were rescued.

By the time the Confederates began responding, the damage was already done and the gunboats were leaving. Most of the men who were rescued on this raid immediately joined the Union Army to fight for their own freedom.

Ben and his family are fictitious characters, but Minus Hamilton, an 88-year-old slave on the Charles Lowndes plantation, told his account of the raid to

Thomas Wentworth Higginson, the colonel of the First South Carolina, another black regiment in the Civil War.

Years later, Tubman also gave her account of the raid to Sarah Bradford, who wrote Tubman's biography.

—*RHR*

LOOKING FURTHER

Adams, Virginia M., ed. *On the Altar of Freedom: A Black Soldier's Civil War Letters From the Front: Corporal James Henry Gooding.* New York: Warner Books, Inc., 1992.

Apthorp, William Lee. *Montgomery's Raids in Florida, Georgia, and South Carolina.* (Typescript in possession of the historical Museum of Southern Florida; Miami, Florida.), ca. 1864. URL: http://www.unf.edu/floridahistoryonline/Projects/Montgomery.html (accessed 6/18/2010).

Bradford, Sarah H. *Harriet: The Moses of Her People*, electronic edition. New York: George R. Lockwood and Son, 1886 URL: http://docsouth.unc.edu/neh/harriet/harriet.html (accessed 6/21/2010).

Bradford, Sarah H. *Scenes in the Life of Harriet Tubman*, electronic edition. Auburn, NY: W.J. Moses, Printer, 1869. URL: http://docsouth.unc.edu/neh/bradford/bradford.html (accessed 6/21/2010).

Canant, Judy, et. al. *The Civil War in South Carolina: Colleton District Property Losses of Record*, 2001. URL: http://sciway3.net/clark/civilwar/ColletonDistLosses.html (accessed 6/18/2010).

"Colonel James Montgomery's Late Raid." *Semi-Weekly Wisconsin.* 26 June 1863: 1. URL: http://newspaperarchive.com/semi-weekly-wisconsin/1863-06-26/page-1 (accessed 5/15/2013).

Conrad, Earl. *General Tubman: Campaign on the Combahee.* Washington, D.C.: Associated Publishers, Inc., 1986. URL: http://www.harriettubman.com/tubman2.html (accessed 6/18/2010).

"Conservation of Historical Resources: Proposed Combahee Ferry Historic District." South Carolina Department of Transportation. 2008 URL: http://www.scdot.org/environmental-stewardship/ferry.shtml (accessed 6/18/2010).

"Dis Un and Dat Un." Live storytelling performances by James David "Sparky" Rucker Jr., 1987-present. (He learned this story from Bessie Jones of the Georgia Sea Island Singers.)

"Enemy's Raid on the Banks of the Combahee." *The Charleston Mercury.* 4 June 1863. URL: http://www.cw-chronicles.com/blog/the-enemy%e2%80%99s-raid-on-the-banks-of-the-combahee/ (accessed 6/19/2010).

Gladstone, William A. *Men of Color.* Gettysburg, PA: Thomas Publications, 1993.

Hughes, Langston and Arna Bontemps, eds. *The Book of Negro Folklore.* New York: Dodd, Mead & Co., 1958.

Hurston, Zora Neale. *Every Tongue Got to Confess: Negro Folk-Tales from the Gulf States.* New York: Harper Collins Publishers Inc., 2001.

Kalman, Bobbie. *Historic Communities: Life on a Plantation.* New York: Crabtree Publishing Co., 1997.

Larson, Kate Clifford. *Bound for the Promised Land: Harriet Tubman – Portrait of an American Hero.* New York: One World Ballantine Books, 2004.

Looby, Christopher, ed. *The Complete Civil War Journal and Selected Letters of Thomas Wentworth Higginson.* Chicago and London: University of Chicago Press, 2000.

Paras, Andy. "Bridge Brings Focus on Tubman: Combahee River Span to Honor Woman's Work." *The Post and Courier.* 20 February 2006: 1B+. URL: http://www.harriettubman.com/bridge.html (accessed 6/18/2010).

Petry, Ann. *Harriet Tubman: Conductor on the Underground Railroad*. New York: Simon and Schuster, Inc., 1955.

"Raid Among the Rice Plantations" (brief excerpt from *Harper's Weekly*, 4 July 1863). URL: http://www.heritagelib.org/articles/the-raid-on-the-combahee (accessed 6/19/2010).

"Raid Among the Rice Plantations" (includes Surgeon Robinson's report with link to illustration). *Harper's Weekly*. 4 July 1863: 427. URL: http://www.sonofthesouth.net/leefoundation/civil-war/1863/july/battle-millikens-bend.htm (accessed 6/19/2010).

"Raid of Second South Carolina Volunteers (Col. Montgomery) Among the Rice Plantations on the Combahee, S.C." (illustration). *Harper's Weekly*. 4 July 1863: 429. URL: http://www.sonofthesouth.net/leefoundation/civil-war/1863/july/whipped-slave.htm (accessed 6/19/2010).

"Reading 1: Rice Cultivation in Georgetown County." National Park Service. URL: http://www.nps.gov/history/nr/twhp/ww-wlps/lessons/3rice/3facts1.htm (accessed 6/18/2010).

Rucker, James David "Sparky" Jr. *A Rucker Family History*. (unpublished)

Sterling, Dorothy. *The Story of Harriet Tubman: Freedom Train*. New York: Scholastic, Inc., 1954.

Taylor, M.W. *Harriet Tubman: Antislavery Activist*. New York: Chelsea House Publishers, 1991.

U.S. Census Bureau. "1850 United States Federal Census." Washington DC: Government Printing Office.

U.S. Census Bureau. "1860 United States Federal Census." Washington DC: Government Printing Office.

The War of the Rebellion: A Compilation of the Official Records of the Union and Confederate Armies. Series I, Vol. XIV. Washington D.C.: Government Printing Office, 1885.

Washington, Wayne. "Forgotten Mission of Liberation: Work Uncovers Site Where Raid Freed 700 Slaves." *The State*. 16 October 2005: A1. URL: http://www.diaspora.uiuc.edu/news1205/news1205.html (accessed 6/18/2010).